Introducing Microsoft Purview

Unlocking the Power of Governance, Compliance, and Security in the Modern Cloud Enterprise

Charles Waghmare

Apress®

Introducing Microsoft Purview: Unlocking the Power of Governance, Compliance, and Security in the Modern Cloud Enterprise

Charles Waghmare
Matunga Mumbai, Maharashtra, India

ISBN-13 (pbk): 979-8-8688-1203-3   ISBN-13 (electronic): 979-8-8688-1204-0
https://doi.org/10.1007/979-8-8688-1204-0

Copyright © 2025 by Charles Waghmare

Managing Director, Apress Media LLC: Welmoed Spahr
Acquisitions Editor: Smriti Srivastava
Editorial Assistant: Kripa Joseph

Cover designed by eStudioCalamar

Cover image designed by Pixabay

Distributed to the book trade worldwide by Springer Science+Business Media New York, 1 New York Plaza, Suite 4600, New York, NY 10004-1562, USA. Phone 1-800-SPRINGER, fax (201) 348-4505, e-mail orders-ny@springer-sbm.com, or visit www.springeronline.com. Apress Media, LLC is a California LLC and the sole member (owner) is Springer Science + Business Media Finance Inc (SSBM Finance Inc). SSBM Finance Inc is a **Delaware** corporation.

For information on translations, please e-mail booktranslations@springernature.com; for reprint, paperback, or audio rights, please e-mail bookpermissions@springernature.com.

Apress titles may be purchased in bulk for academic, corporate, or promotional use. eBook versions and licenses are also available for most titles. For more information, reference our Print and eBook Bulk Sales web page at http://www.apress.com/bulk-sales.

Any source code or other supplementary material referenced by the author in this book is available to readers on GitHub. For more detailed information, please visit https://www.apress.com/gp/services/source-code.

If disposing of this product, please recycle the paper

The law of the LORD is perfect, converting the soul:
the testimony of the LORD is sure, making wise
the simple.

—Psalms 19:7

First, I would like to say thanks to Almighty Lord Jesus Christ for offering me yet another opportunity to author this book. I completely owe everything to Him. I take this opportunity to praise and glorify Lord Christ for all the wonderful things that He has been doing in my life. God bless.

My Dedication:

While approaching the second death anniversary of my dearest mother, late Mrs. Kamala David Waghmare, I have begun writing this book. I dedicate this book to my dearest mother and to my father, Mr. David Genu Waghmare, who both laid foundation of my life and career. Without them, I am nothing. I thank God for the best mom and dad.

Also, I dedicate this book to my adorable wife, Mrs. Priya Waghmare, for her support, love, encouragement, and care.

Table of Contents

About the Author

Charles David Waghmare, a DBA (Doctor of Business Administration) scholar from the prestigious SP Jain School of Global Management and an MBA from the same prestigious B-School, has over 17 years of industry experience in IT, engineering, and energy sectors.

Charles is presently working with a global energy leader since 2019 as an information management consultant in the Microsoft 365 space. Before that, he worked for Capgemini for eight years in various roles including Viva Engage community manager and manager of the Drupal-based Enterprise Knowledge Management system. He also developed a knowledge management platform for Capgemini's Digital Customer Experience (DCX) organization using SharePoint Online to manage client references and knowledge assets related to artificial intelligence and customer experience (CX). Further, he adopted Microsoft Azure chatbots to automate communication channels with the customers.

Charles also worked for ATOS (erstwhile SIEMENS Information Systems Limited) for five years. During his tenure there, he was a community manager of SAP-based communities, where he utilized Technoweb 2.0 – a Viva Engage-like platform – and on-premises SharePoint to manage SAP user-based communities. Also, Charles was the global rollout manager for a structured document management system built in on-premises SharePoint.

Charles has penned several books on Microsoft 365 technologies such as Viva Engage, SharePoint Online, and Azure chatbots and on ChatGPT. Further, he loves reading motivational books in his spare time, his favorite being *The Monk Who Sold His Ferrari*, *The 5 AM Club*, and *The Everyday Hero Manisfesto*.

About the Technical Reviewer

Kasam Shaikh is a prominent figure in India's artificial intelligence landscape, holding the distinction of being one of the country's first four Microsoft Most Valuable Professionals (MVPs) in AI. Currently serving as a senior architect at Capgemini, Kasam boasts an impressive track record as an author, having authored five best-selling books dedicated to Azure and AI technologies. Beyond his writing endeavors, Kasam is recognized as a Microsoft Certified Trainer (MCT) and influential tech YouTuber (@mekasamshaikh). He also leads the largest online Azure AI community, known as DearAzure I Azure INDIA, and is a globally renowned AI speaker. His commitment to knowledge sharing extends to contributions to Microsoft Learn, where he plays a pivotal role.

Within the realm of AI, Kasam is a respected subject matter expert (SME) in generative AI for the cloud, complementing his role as a chief architect. He actively promotes the adoption of No Code and Azure OpenAI solutions and possesses a strong foundation in hybrid and cross-cloud practices. Kasam Shaikh's versatility and expertise make him an invaluable asset in the rapidly evolving landscape of technology, contributing significantly to the advancement of Azure and AI.

In summary, Kasam Shaikh is a multifaceted professional who excels in both technical expertise and knowledge dissemination. His contributions span writing, training, community leadership, public speaking, and architecture, establishing him as a true luminary in the world of Azure and AI.

Acknowledgments

I would like to acknowledge the following people who are close to my heart:

Late Mr. Anil Malvankar, ex-DGM at SIEMENS, who offered me my first job at SIEMENS. I thank for his mentoring until his last day on the earth, 28th April 2024.

Late Mr. Alwin Fernandis, my beloved friend. He is not present with me today, but his memories will exist in my heart forever.

Mr. Sridhar "Sri" Maheswar, supply chain consultant, NNIT. I am always grateful for your support, my beloved friend.

Mr. Pravin V. Thorat, Head of India Operations at ATOS. I thank you for your prayers and good wishes.

CHAPTER 1

Introduction to Microsoft Purview

Microsoft Purview is a comprehensive suite of data governance and compliance tools designed to help organizations manage, protect, and gain insights from their data across various environments. Launched as part of Microsoft's broader strategy to address the growing complexities of data management in hybrid and multicloud environments, Purview provides a unified platform that integrates data cataloging, data lineage, and data classification with robust governance and compliance capabilities.

Besides managing data, Microsoft Purview is also focused on compliance and governance. It has a robust set of tools that can be used to enforce policies and ensure that organizations follow regulations such as HIPAA, GDPR, and CCPA. The platform's reporting features are additionally helpful in demonstrating compliance. One of the most critical features of Microsoft Purview is its ability to monitor and manage the data lineage. This feature allows organizations to identify and analyze the various systems that collect and store their data. It helps them ensure that their data is secure and that they are able to perform effective troubleshooting.

With the ability to integrate with other Microsoft offerings, such as Power BI and Azure Analytics, Microsoft Purview can help organizations establish a comprehensive data governance strategy. Thus, this ensures that the platform can serve as the central hub for any organization's

© Charles Waghmare 2025
C. Waghmare, *Introducing Microsoft Purview*,
https://doi.org/10.1007/979-8-8688-1204-0_1

data management. The flexible and powerful Microsoft Purview data management platform is ideal for organizations that want to improve the efficiency and effectiveness of their data operations. It can help them manage their data assets while ensuring that they are compliant and secure. As the volume of data continues to increase, it will become even more important that organizations have the necessary tools to keep up with the changes.

In this introductory chapter, we aim to provide overview of Microsoft Purview features, capabilities such as data discovery and classification, data cataloging, data lineage, data governance, data sharing and collaboration, data privacy and security, and other features of Microsoft Purview. Further, we will look into architecture and core components such as information catalog, information map, information insights, and information policies.

Note   Theoretically, there is a difference between the manner in which a piece of data and information is defined. In this book, we will sometimes prefer using the word information over data to accurately fix context; however, this setting does not determine the application to the way a piece of data is defined, and application of topics in this book will be equally deemed fit wherever it applies to data as well. Both words will be invariably used however with the scope of identical intended meaning and with a standard business understanding.

Introduction

The Microsoft Purview platform provides comprehensive solutions that help organizations manage and protect their data. These solutions help organizations address the various challenges that data fragmentation and the lack of visibility present in their organizations. The Microsoft Purview platform combines the capabilities of its former Azure platform and 365 Compliance Services with a unified set of solutions designed to help organizations manage their data. Through the Microsoft Purview platform, different teams as shown in Figure 1-1 can gain a deeper understanding of their data and manage it across their entire lifecycle. It also helps them comply with regulations and manage.

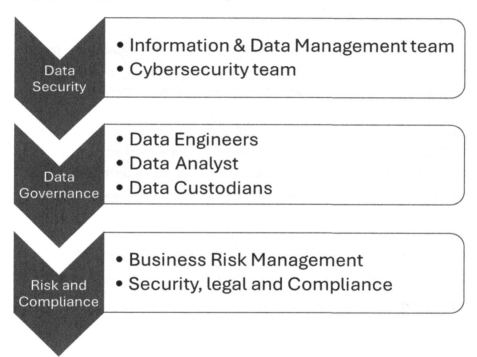

Figure 1-1. *Teams adopting Microsoft Purview*

Key Features of Microsoft Purview

With Microsoft Purview, organizations can now meet the diverse needs of their data management and governance teams. As they continue to expand their operations and collect data across various cloud, on-premises, and software-as-a-service environments, they can realize a comprehensive view of their data at scale. In this section, we will explore the many features of Microsoft Purview, which will enable organizations to enhance their data governance and regulatory compliance efforts.

Comprehensive Information Discovery and Classification

Microsoft Purview's classification and data discovery engine are at the heart of the company's capabilities. Example of information discovery is eDiscovery which is used during legal proceedings to identifying evidence in emails, databases, and other electronic communication medium. On other hand, information can be classified as internal, confidential, and most confidential based on business requirements. Information which is classified as internal can be an intranet site for internal users. Project-specific documents will be classified as confidential as these are for a specific group of people. Customer contacts will be most confidential as companies' reputation depends upon such. In an era where information is spread across various platforms and environments, effective data classification and discovery are critical such as

Automated Information Discovery

- With Microsoft Purview's data discovery tools, organizations can easily identify and analyze data from various sources, such as on-premises databases and software-as-a-service offerings. This feature helps them maintain an updated inventory of their data.

- The Purview platform supports various types of data sources, such as relational databases and cloud-based platforms like Amazon Web Services, Google

Cloud Storage, and Microsoft Azure Blob Storage. This ensures that organizations can catalog and identify all their data regardless of its location.

- Purview can perform incremental scans, which only updates data that have changed since the previous scan. This feature helps organizations keep their data catalog current and reduce their system resources.

Through Microsoft's AI-powered insights, Purview's discovery engine can classify and recognize data according to its content, usage patterns, and context. This method ensures that new information is properly categorized.

Information Classification

When it comes to understanding an organization's data, classification plays a vital role. This is especially true when handling sensitive information which is explained as below.

- Microsoft Purview has built-in classifiers that can automatically identify various types of data. These include financial information, protected health information, and intellectual property. These tools can help organizations quickly find the location of sensitive data.

- Due to the unique nature of an organization's data, it is often necessary to create custom classification tools that are specific to the organization. Through Purview, an organization can identify the types of data that it needs to classify. These tools can be customized to recognize specific keywords or patterns.

- Classification automatically tags data with labels that highlight its ownership, type, and sensitivity. These labels can help improve the discoverability of information in the catalog and comply with various regulations.

5

Centralized Data Cataloging

Microsoft Purview's centralized data catalog is the hub of the platform, serving as a single point of reference that holds all the company's data assets with unified data cataloging. Examples of data cataloguing could be for a given data set of cities whether one can group them based on country business where enterprise exists.

Unified Data Catalog

A comprehensive data catalog is essential for managing the massive amount of information that an organization has stored in various environments. With Microsoft Purview's catalog, you can easily consolidate all of your discovered data into a single repository, giving you a holistic view of the data landscape.

- The catalog's metadata management features capture and store details about each type of data asset, such as its structure, classification, lineage, and source. These provide valuable context to help you understand their quality and relevance.

- The Purview catalog can also integrate with business glossaries and data schemas, which help users understand the concepts of data in a more business-oriented manner. This feature helps nontechnical users gain access to the information they need.

- Users can easily search the contents of the Purview data catalog using various filters, such as source, owner, data type, and sensitivity. Its search capabilities are designed to provide relevant results in a fast and efficient manner, especially in large-scale data sets.

Data Asset Enrichment

In addition to basic metadata, the Purview platform also allows users to enrich their data assets with additional details, which helps improve their governance and usability with below:

- Purview's annotations feature allows users to add their own annotations to their data assets, which provide instructions on how to interpret and use the information. They can also be used to share knowledge across teams.

- The Purview data catalog can also assign one or both a steward and an owner to each asset. The latter is responsible for ensuring that the data follows policies, while the former is accountable for its relevance and accuracy. This process helps establish a clear understanding of the responsibilities related to data management.

- Purview's usage analytics feature can help users identify the activities and usage of their data assets. This information can be utilized to improve the efficiency of data management and ensure that it is readily accessible to those who need it.

Data Lineage and Impact Analysis

One of the most critical factors that organizations need to consider when it comes to tracing the flow of data is understanding the data lineage. This feature allows them to identify the various sources of their data and ensure that it is secure. With Microsoft Purview, they can easily view and analyze the data lineage.

End-to-End Data Lineage

Through Purview, organizations can visualize and capture the entire journey of their data, from its initial source to its destination. This feature provides a comprehensive view of how data is transformed and aggregated across various systems.

- Users can explore the data's journey using interactive lineage diagrams, which highlight the various steps involved in the data's transformation, such as data warehouses, ETL pipelines, and business intelligence tools. These tools make it easier to identify areas of weakness or potential bottlenecks.

- The ability to track and record the transformation process ensures that data is accurately stored and analyzed. This feature is very important for ensuring that the changes are performed properly and that the data is not affected by any issues.

- With the ability to map the sources and targets of data, users can easily identify where and how it is being consumed. This feature helps organizations keep track of their data's flow and ensure that they are able to maintain transparency.

Impact Analysis

An impact analysis is a must-have for organizations that require a deeper understanding of how changes in their data sets can affect them.

- Users can simulate the effect of changes to data structures, transformations, and sources through Purview's change impact assessment. This tool helps organizations identify potential disruptions that could affect their downstream systems and reports.

- The Purview feature can visualize the dependencies between various processes and data assets, which can help identify areas where changes can affect them. This is particularly useful in complex environments where multiple data sources are interconnected.

Robust Data Governance

The core of Microsoft Purview's capabilities is data governance, which enables organizations to manage and enforce policies. It provides them with the necessary tools to comply with regulations and legal requirements. Example of data governance includes retention of data such as information labeled as records based on country jurisdiction and removal of personal data such as Passport document, health checkup document from company repositories.

Policy Management and Enforcement

Data governance is a process that involves the creation, implementation, and enforcement of policies that regulate how information is accessed, utilized, and safeguarded.

- Through the use of Purview, organizations can create and enforce policies that specify the types of data assets that can be accessed and what conditions are required to safeguard them. These policies can then be applied across the enterprise to ensure consistency.

- With the help of Purview, organizations can create and enforce policies that specify the types of data assets that can be accessed and what conditions are required to safeguard them. These policies can then be applied across the enterprise to ensure consistency.

- Through the creation of custom policies, organizations can address various issues related to data quality and security. These can then be enforced across the enterprise.

Role-Based Access Control (RBAC)

Through the integration of Purview with Azure Active Directory, it can provide a role-based access control solution that ensures that only authorized individuals can access sensitive data.

- The use of a granular permissions approach allows organizations to set detailed permissions for specific users based on their roles, which helps prevent unauthorized access and ensures data security.

- The ability to assign permissions in a hierarchical manner allows for intricate role structures that reflect the needs of an organization. This flexibility enables the development of policies that are tailored to the varying levels of the company.

Enhanced Compliance Management

The comprehensive tools included in Microsoft Purview help organizations comply with the internal and external regulations. Examples of compliance adherence are Health Insurance Portability and Accountability Act of 1996 (HIPAA), the General Data Protection Regulation (GDPR),

Regulatory Compliance Support

In regulated industries, companies must abide by various laws and regulations when it comes to handling information. With Purview, they can easily comply with these requirements.

- Purview also includes built-in templates for various regulatory frameworks, like the Health Insurance Portability and Accountability Act of 1996 (HIPAA), the General Data Protection Regulation (GDPR), and the CCPA. These predefined policies and controls can help organizations simplify their compliance efforts.

- Additionally, companies can utilize custom controls to address specific internal policies or regulatory requirements. These can be enforced throughout the organization and ensure consistent compliance.

- With the ability to create detailed reports on demand, Purview helps organizations comply with regulations. These reports can be used by internal auditors to demonstrate that an organization is following the regulations.

Audit Trails and Logging

A thorough record of how data is used, accessed, and enforced is essential for proper accountability and compliance.

- With the ability to generate comprehensive audit logs, Purview can track every aspect of the data's lifecycle, such as the actions taken, policies enforced, and transformations. This ensures that an organization follows proper security and compliance procedures.

11

- Tools for analyzing audit logs are included in Purview, allowing organizations to find patterns, identify anomalies, and generate insight from their data. This process can also help with improving governance practices and ensuring that their compliance procedures are in order.

- The ability to create real-time visibility into an organization's compliance posture is also a feature of Purview's compliance dashboards. These allow stakeholders to monitor the status of the company's compliance program and take immediate action to address any issues.

Data Sharing and Collaboration

One of the most critical factors that businesses consider when it comes to data management is the ability to share information. With Microsoft Purview, they can ensure that their data is protected and managed in a secure manner. Example is that the external users can access company information based on authentication such as one-time password.

Internal Data Sharing

Through Microsoft Purview, organizations can easily share and manage their internal data. It enables secure collaboration and access to this data.

- Microsoft Purview's access control policy ensures that only authorized users can access the company's data. This helps prevent unauthorized access and safeguard sensitive information.

- With the help of data sharing agreements, Microsoft Purview can help organizations create a framework that enables them to share and manage their internal information. These agreements can be designed to specify the conditions under which this data can be shared.

- Microsoft Purview also helps organizations create collaboration spaces that allow teams to work together on projects related to data. These types of environments can be used to access and manage data while maintaining strict governance policies.

External Data Sharing

Most organizations need to share information with external suppliers, customers, or partners. With the help of Microsoft Purview, they can protect their data assets through secure data exchange.

- Purview offers a secure method for organizations to distribute information to external partners. This method is carried out through data sharing agreements and access control policies, with the stipulation that recipients should only be authorized.

- When it comes to sharing sensitive information with other parties, Purview supports masking techniques, which hide the details of the data. This ensures that the information is not exposed to confidential details.

- With the help of data sharing agreements, Microsoft Purview can help organizations monitor and track the activities of their partners and external suppliers. This ensures that they are following proper guidelines and that the information they are sharing is secure.

Advanced Data Privacy and Security

One of the most critical factors that businesses consider when it comes to protecting their data is having the proper security and privacy controls. With Microsoft Purview, they can easily manage and secure their sensitive data. Also, one can apply sensitive labels such as confidential, internal, and most confidential.

Sensitive Data Protection

With the help of Purview's data protection capabilities, organizations can easily identify and secure their sensitive information. This ensures that they follow proper security policies and regulations.

- With Purview's classification engine, you can easily identify sensitive information such as health records, financial information, and PII (Personal Information Identity). This process is the first step in implementing suitable security measures to safeguard your data.

- Through its integration with Azure's encryption services, Purview can now provide end-to-end protection for sensitive data. This ensures that it's protected even if it's accessed or intercepted without authorization.

- With the help of its role-based access control features, Purview can now provide organizations with strict access controls that prevent unauthorized users from accessing and manipulating sensitive data. These can be based on various factors such as the sensitivity level of the data, the role of the users, and the business needs of the organization.

14

Data Masking and Obfuscation

Obfuscation and data masking are important techniques when it comes to protecting sensitive information, especially in environments where the data is required to be shared or utilized for nonproduction purposes.

- Purview supports the use of static data masking, a method that permanently hides sensitive information in nonproduction settings, such as training and development. This ensures that the data is not exposed while the activity takes place.

- Another type of data masking that Purview supports is dynamic data masking. This method can be used to protect sensitive information at runtime without affecting its underlying structure. It's ideal for environments where the data needs to be kept secure while still being used for certain operations.

- With the ability to create custom rules, organizations can easily protect their sensitive information by implementing a flexible approach to protecting it. This can be done by implementing rules for various data types.

Integration with Microsoft Ecosystem

The Microsoft Purview platform is designed to work seamlessly with other Microsoft services and products. It provides a cohesive experience for companies that depend on the company's ecosystem. For example, deletion and retention of files in SharePoint and MS Teams can be configured from Microsoft Purview.

Azure Synapse Analytics Integration

The Microsoft Azure Synapse Analytics platform is a powerful tool for analyzing and managing big data. Through its integration with Purview, organizations can now have a unified view of their data.

- With the ability to enforce policies across multiple Synapse Analytics environments, Purview helps organizations improve the quality of their data.

- Through the integration of Purview, organizations can now gain a deeper understanding of how their data is consumed and transformed in the analytics process. This information helps ensure that the outputs of the analytics are reliable and accurate.

- The integration of Purview's catalog with the Synapse platform allows users to easily find and manage their data assets. This ensures that their data is always accessible and governed in a consistent manner across both platforms.

Power BI Integration

With the ability to create interactive dashboards and reports, Power BI is a powerful tool for analyzing and managing business data. The integration of Purview and Power BI will help organizations improve the governance of their data.

- With the ability to govern and manage the content of Power BI's data assets, such as reports and dashboards, Purview helps ensure that the information is secure, conforms to company policies, and is accurate.

- Purview's data lineage for Power BI reports provides detailed information about the data sources and transformations performed in the final reports. This helps users understand how their reports were made and ensure that they are accurate.

- Companies can now enforce and apply data protection policies in Power BI through the integration of Purview's sensitivity labels. This ensures that sensitive information is handled properly in reports and dashboards.

Microsoft 365 Integration

The Microsoft 365 suite of productivity tools includes services such as Exchange, SharePoint, and OneDrive. Through its integration with Microsoft 365, Purview can now extend the scope of data governance to the unstructured information stored in these services.

- With the ability to govern and manage the content of Power BI's data assets, such as reports and dashboards, Purview helps ensure that the information is secure, conforms to company policies, and is accurate. This capability is especially important for organizations that need to manage sensitive information.

- With the ability to apply Purview's sensitivity labels to emails and files in Microsoft 365, organizations can now ensure that their sensitive content is protected from unauthorized access and manipulation. This helps prevent data leaks and ensures that their privacy policies are followed.

- With the ability to monitor and audit the activities of Microsoft 365, organizations can now keep track of how their data is being used and accessed by other employees. This capability is very important to ensure that their operations are following proper policies and that their data is secure.

Data Quality Management

High-quality data is essential for making informed decisions and reporting. With Microsoft Purview, you can manage and improve the data quality of your organization. Example includes removal of unwanted data from business data.

Data Quality Metrics

With Microsoft Purview, organizations can easily create and monitor data quality metrics, which can be used to measure the quality of their information.

- The quality dimensions in Microsoft Purview allow organizations to track and analyze the various aspects of their data quality, such as timeliness, completeness, accuracy, and consistency. This lets them identify areas where their data could be improved.

- In addition, Purview supports the creation and monitoring of quality thresholds, which can trigger warnings when the data falls below certain standards. These alerts can help organizations take immediate action to address issues related to data quality.

- Microsoft Purview also has a variety of quality dashboards that provide a comprehensive view of the data quality of an organization. These dashboards help organizations identify areas where they can improve their data quality.

Data Quality Rules and Validation

In order to enforce quality standards, Purview can help organizations create rules for data assets.

- Companies can customize their data quality rules to conform to their specific business needs. These rules can be utilized to ensure that the data meets predefined quality requirements.

- With the help of automatic validation, Purview can also ensure that the data quality rules are applied to the right data assets. This ensures that only high-quality information is used in the operations of the organization.

- Microsoft Purview has a feature that provides a set of workflows that help users resolve issues related to data quality. These help them identify and fix the issues that cause the data quality problems.

Data Quality Monitoring

Keeping track of the quality of data is important for organizations to maintain high standards. With the help of tools in Purview, users can continuously monitor their data quality.

- Purview also supports real-time monitoring, which allows organizations to respond to issues related to data quality immediately. This feature is ideal for monitoring the quality of data assets that have a significant impact on an organization's operations.

- Purview's historical tracking feature allows users to gain a deeper understanding of the data quality by providing insights into its evolution. This feature can also inform the development of data management strategies.

- Through its integration with data pipelines, Purview can now monitor the quality of data at every stage of the process. This ensures that the issues are identified and resolved as soon as possible to minimize the impact on the downstream systems.

Extensibility and Customization

The flexible and adaptable Microsoft Purview platform lets organizations customize it to meet their specific data governance needs. Examples of setting up information policies, such as information disposal for a custom application, can be done through Purview.

Custom Connectors and Integrations

With the ability to create custom connectors and add-ons, Purview lets organizations extend their existing infrastructure to new environments.

- Through the creation of custom connectors, organizations can easily bring nonsupported data sources into Purview. This ensures that all data can be governed using the platform.

- Through the use of the Purview REST APIs, organizations can easily integrate their existing systems and tools into their data governance processes. This ensures that the platform can work seamlessly with other data platforms.

- Through the use of third-party integrations, Purview can now work seamlessly with various data platforms and tools. These tools can help organizations improve their data governance and allow them to take advantage of their existing investments.

Customization of Governance Policies

Organizations have varying requirements when it comes to data governance. With the ability to customize policies, Purview can help them meet these needs.

- Purview's ability to create custom policies allows organizations to implement procedures that are specific to their unique requirements. These can be applied across an organization to ensure consistent enforcement.

- Purview can also help organizations automate the enforcement of policies, which can help them keep their operations running smoothly. This eliminates the need for manual labor and allows them to focus on their core business.

- With the ability to create custom workflows, Purview can help organizations implement procedures that are specific to their operational processes. These can then be integrated into daily operations to improve consistency and efficiency.

Scalability and Performance

The Microsoft Purview platform is designed to handle the demands of large organizations with complex data estates. For example, it covers information management of entire M365 space such as SharePoint Online, Teams, and others.

Scalability

With the ability to handle massive amounts of data, Purview is ideal for organizations that need to find, classify, and manage their data.

- With the ability to handle both horizontal and vertical scalability, Purview can accommodate the increasing complexity and volume of data that an organization encounters. This ensures that it can remain effective in demanding environments.

- One of Purview's most important features is its multiregion support, which allows organizations to manage their data in different regions. This feature is especially beneficial for organizations that have operations in multiple countries.

- The Purview architecture allows the platform to dynamically allocate resources to ensure that it can adapt to changes in workload demands. This helps keep performance up during peak usage periods.

Performance Optimization

Performance optimization is also included in Purview to help organizations achieve efficient data classification and lineage tracking.

- Through the use of advanced scanning algorithms, Purview can reduce the impact on the system's resources during the discovery and classification process. This ensures that scans are performed efficiently and quickly in large-scale data environments.

- One of the most important features of Purview is its support for parallel processing, which allows the platform to perform various tasks at the same time. This allows organizations to reduce the time it takes to process their massive data sets.

- Through the use of indexing and caching techniques, Purview can enhance the efficiency of its data searches and queries. These methods can reduce the time it takes to retrieve lineage information and metadata, allowing organizations to gain quick access to critical business insights.

Concluding this section with Microsoft Purview key features, organizations can easily and effectively manage their data. Its advanced features, such as data discovery and classification, provide them with the necessary tools to ensure that their data is secure and compliant. It also helps them unlock the value of their data by allowing them to make informed decisions and improve their efficiency. Integrating seamlessly with Microsoft's ecosystem, Purview caters to the diverse requirements of companies in different industries, allowing them to stay compliant, secure, and competitive.

An Overview of Microsoft Purview Architecture and Its Core Components

The Microsoft Purview platform is built on a modular and scalable architecture that can be used to build applications and manage various components. It utilizes cloud-native technologies for improved performance and flexibility. It can run on various hybrid platforms, such as Amazon Web Services, Google Cloud, and Azure.

The Purview platform's architecture is composed of various core architectural layers. These can be used to create and manage applications. It can run on various hybrid platforms, such as Amazon Web Services, Google Cloud, and Azure. The data sources layer is composed of various databases, storage, and systems. Through its connectors, Purview can access these sources and catalog, categorize, and discover data. The processing and ingestion layer is responsible for the processing and ingestion of metadata from sources. It includes various mechanisms for lineage tracking, classification, and scanning.

The governance and metadata layer is where the central functions of Purview reside. It includes the information map, information insights, and information catalog. It also provides various governance capabilities, such as compliance controls and policy management. The integration and extension layer are a part of the Purview platform that enables third-party developers to integrate and extend its capabilities with Microsoft products, such as Power BI and Azure. It also provides access to custom connectors and tools.

Below are some core components of Microsoft purview which includes information catalog, information map, information insights, and information policies.

Information Catalog

Microsoft Purview's information catalog is a repository that stores all the details about an organization's data assets. It enables organizations to easily find, understand, and manage their data.

- The information catalog's metadata management features capture and organize information about each data asset's structure, classification, ownership, and source. This helps organizations understand their data's quality and context.

- The information catalog can be used to automate the discovery of data assets in various cloud, on-premises, and SaaS environments. It can handle diverse types of data, such as structured and unstructured information.

- The information catalog's navigation features allow users to quickly find and analyze the details about their data assets. Its search capabilities are designed to provide organizations with the necessary information to make informed decisions.

- In addition to standard metadata, the information catalog also allows users to enrich their data by adding annotations, metrics, and business terms. This can help improve the governance and usability of the data.

Information Map

The information map is a visual representation of an organization's data landscape. It shows how information flows across various processes and systems. This helps organizations identify the dependencies and lineage of their data as follows.

- The information map provides end-to-end representation of the data lineage, showing how information traverses from its source to its destination. This enables organizations to understand how changes affect the lineage of their data and identify their origins.

- The information map displays the dependencies between various systems, processes, and data assets. This helps organizations identify potential issues and gain a better understanding of their data's interconnections.

- An impact analysis can be performed by analyzing the information map. It allows organizations to determine the effects of changes on various systems, data sources, or processes. This can be useful in planning and implementing changes to policies or migration.

- Users can explore the details of a particular data asset or procedure through the interactive exploration feature of the information map. This lets them gain a deeper understanding of their complex data environment and make more informed decisions regarding governance and management.

Information Insights

Microsoft Purview's information insights component offers reporting and analytical capabilities. This tool helps organizations assess their governance practices, data landscape, and compliance stance explained as below.

- Reports and dashboards about an organization's compliance with internal and regulatory policies can be found in information insights. These reports help the user identify areas of concern and monitor the status of their compliance.

- The data usage analytics feature can help organizations identify the usage patterns of their data assets. It can also provide insight into the possible bottlenecks and trends that affect their data access. This helps them improve their data management techniques and ensure that they can access high-value information.

- The quality monitoring feature in information insights can help organizations monitor the overall health of their data. It can analyze the various dimensions of data quality, such as completeness and accuracy.

- Through the ability to create custom reports, organizations can customize the reports to meet their specific needs. This allows them to focus on the most relevant insights and metrics.

Information Policies

In Microsoft Purview, information policies define the rules and regulations that govern how data is managed, accessed, and secured. These policies are important for ensuring that information is protected and secure.

- The access control policies set the rules and regulations that define who can and should be allowed to access certain data assets. With Azure Active Directory,

Purview can enforce role-based access control to prevent unauthorized individuals from accessing sensitive data.

- Information policies include methods for preserving and discarding data, which ensures that it is stored and handled in accordance with relevant regulations and company standards. Such policies can help organizations manage their information lifecycle and prevent superfluous accumulation.

- Through Purview, organizations can categorize their data assets according to their sensitivity level. These labels help guide the proper handling and safeguarding of sensitive information.

- With the help of Purview's policy automation and enforcement capabilities, organizations can easily implement and enforce information policies. This helps minimize the risk of noncompliance and ensure that the rules are followed consistently.

- Purview also logs all user and access events to keep track of how the company follows its information policies. This feature is useful in monitoring compliance, allowing investigators to review records.

In conclusion, the Microsoft Purview's architecture is designed to provide a powerful and flexible solution for managing information governance. It includes a variety of components, such as an information map, an information catalog, and an information insights platform. These tools help organizations identify and manage their data assets and ensure they are following the regulations. Through its integration with

Microsoft's ecosystem, Purview can help organizations achieve better data governance. It offers a convenient and efficient way to manage their information assets.

With this, we have come to an end to this introductory chapter on Microsoft Purview. In this introductory chapter, we have experienced overview of Microsoft Purview features, capabilities such as data discovery and classification, data cataloging, data lineage, data governance, data sharing and collaboration, data privacy and security, and other features part of Microsoft Purview. Further, we took a peripheral look at the architecture and core components such as information catalog, information map, information insights, and information policies. In the next chapter, we will explore the features of cataloging and metadata management in Microsoft Purview such as creating and managing a centralized information catalog, metadata extraction and enrichment, and integration with various data sources (on-premises, cloud, SaaS).

CHAPTER 2

Introduction to Information Governance in Microsoft Purview

In the previous chapter, we have seen an overview of Microsoft Purview features, capabilities such as data discovery and classification, data cataloging, data lineage, data governance, data sharing and collaboration, data privacy and security, and other features part of Microsoft Purview. Further, we have experienced architecture and core components such as information catalog, information map, information insights, and information policies.

In this chapter, we shall see the introduction of information governance in the Microsoft Purview portal in order to provide a granular approach for information governance in a modern enterprise context. Furthermore, we will be exploring core capabilities of Microsoft Purview around information security, information governance, and risk and compliance.

© Charles Waghmare 2025
C. Waghmare, *Introducing Microsoft Purview*,
https://doi.org/10.1007/979-8-8688-1204-0_2

Introduction

The Microsoft Purview platform provides comprehensive solutions that help organizations manage and protect their data. These solutions help organizations address the various challenges that data fragmentation and the lack of visibility present in their organizations. Through the Microsoft Purview platform, organizations can now address the various challenges of data management and protection. It combines the offerings of Microsoft 365 and Azure.

With the help of the Purview platform, organizations will be able to gain a deeper understanding of their data and manage its various risks. It will also help them protect and manage their data across their entire organization. Information or data security, governance, and compliance together make Microsoft Purview as shown in Figure 2-1.

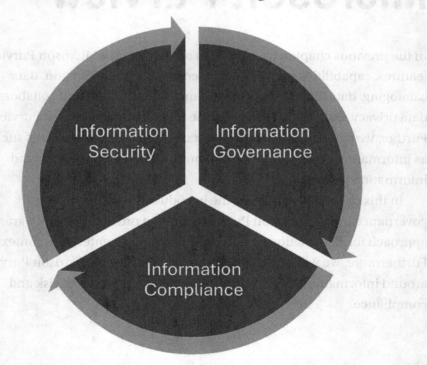

Figure 2-1. *Core components of Microsoft Purview*

With Microsoft Purview, organizations can easily manage and secure their data across all of their data centers. Below is the overview on core components of Microsoft Purview on Microsoft Purview.

Information Security

Through its comprehensive set of security solutions, Microsoft Purview helps organizations identify and secure sensitive information. The information or data security solutions included are shown in Figure 2-2.

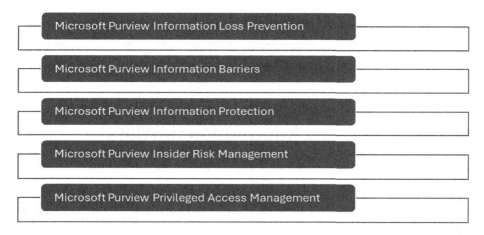

Figure 2-2. *Solution offerings in information security component*

Below is the overview of each of the above solution offerings as shown in Figure 2-2, which are information loss prevention, information barriers, information protection, risk management, and privileged access management.

Microsoft Purview Information Loss Prevention

There are many organizations that have sensitive information that they can control. This includes the data that they collect regarding financial transactions and health records.

To protect this information and to reduce the risk that it will be overshared, organizations need to implement a data loss prevention strategy. This method involves preventing users from sharing it with people that they shouldn't have.

Microsoft Purview can help you implement an information loss prevention strategy. It allows you to define and apply policies that will help prevent sensitive data from being overshared. Windows 10, Windows 11, macOS, and Office 365 services are some of the most common types of applications that are used by organizations. With the help of deep content analysis, Microsoft Purview can identify sensitive items in these types of information. This method is different from traditional text scans.

In order to identify sensitive items in the data, Microsoft Purview uses various methods such as internal function validation, regular expressions, and machine learning algorithms.

Microsoft Purview Information Barriers

Through Microsoft 365, organizations can collaborate and communicate with their various users across different groups. It also supports ways to limit the number of people communicating and working together in certain areas to avoid conflicts of interest. This can also apply to situations where there are certain people who need to be restricted from working together and communicating with each other to protect the company's internal information.

In addition to being able to restrict the number of people working together and communicating with each other, Microsoft also supports policies that prevent the spread of confidential information. These policies can be used by a compliance administrator to prevent the activities of certain groups within Microsoft Teams. Individuals within the day trader group should not be able to share or communicate with the marketing team. In the same school district, instructors should not be able to share files with students. On the other hand, finance personnel should not be able to communicate with other groups within the company using confidential information.

Members of an internal team that has trade secrets should avoid using the company's online platforms to communicate with other users in certain groups. Similarly, research teams should only use the platform to talk to development personnel. Steps used in information barriers are shown in Figure 2-3.

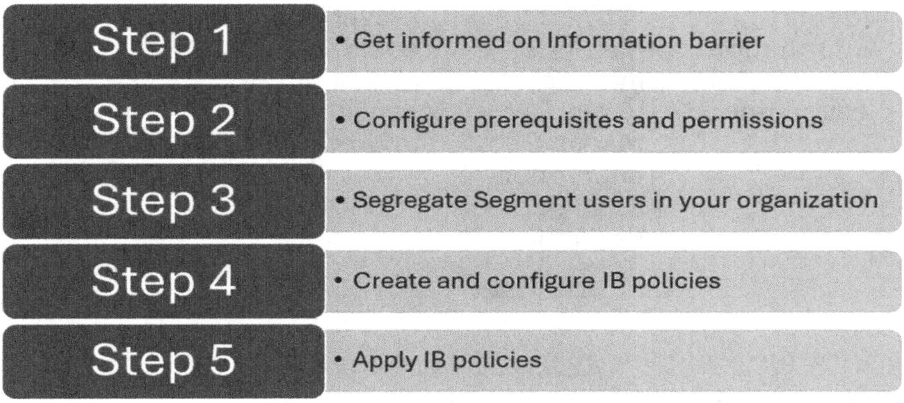

Figure 2-3. *Steps used in information barriers*

Microsoft Purview Information Protection

Microsoft Purview information protection suite provides tools that help organizations identify, classify, and safeguard sensitive data. These capabilities which are powered by intelligent platform allow them to protect their information in various ways as explained in Figure 2-4.

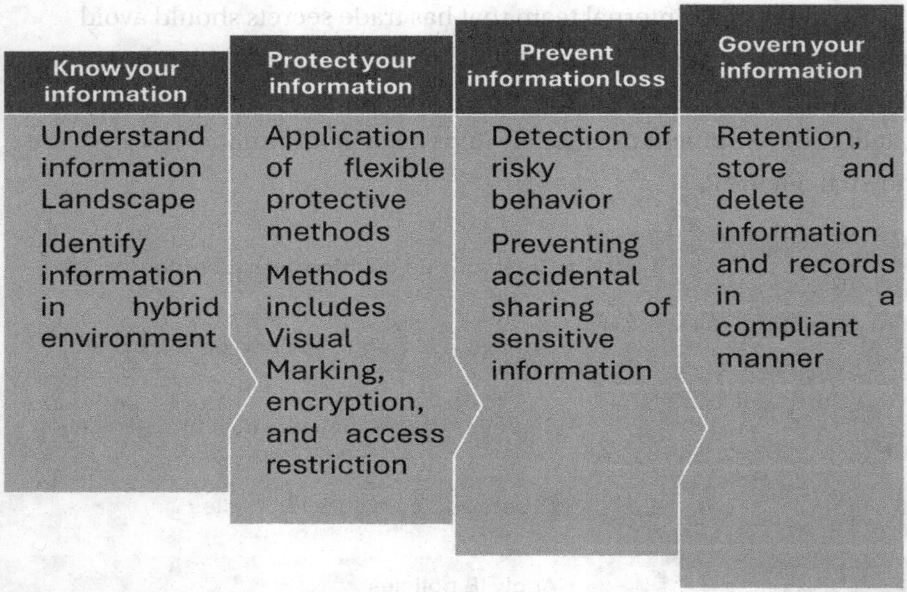

Know your information	Protect your information	Prevent information loss	Govern your information
Understand information Landscape Identify information in hybrid environment	Application of flexible protective methods Methods includes Visual Marking, encryption, and access restriction	Detection of risky behavior Preventing accidental sharing of sensitive information	Retention, store and delete information and records in a compliant manner

Figure 2-4. *Capabilities in information protection*

Know Your Information

Use these capabilities to identify and understand the sensitive data residing in your hybrid environment.

Capability	Type of problem to which solution exists
Sensitive information types	Built-in or custom functions or expressions can be used to identify sensitive information. Corroborative proof can also include proximity, keywords, and confidence levels
Trainable classifiers	Instead of finding patterns in an item, you can use examples of information that you're interested in to identify sensitive information. You can train a classifier using built-in features or your own content

(*continued*)

Capability	Type of problem to which solution exists
Information classification	A graphical representation of an organization's products that have retention or sensitivity labels can help identify those items. It can also help you understand the actions of your users when it comes to these items

Protect Your Information

These capabilities can be used to implement various protection measures such as visual markings, access restrictions, and encryption.

Capability	Type of problem to which solution exists
Sensitivity labels	The goal of this solution is to provide a single labeling solution that enables organizations to protect their data as it travels across their various devices and apps. It can be used to manage sensitive labels for Office apps and email, encrypt documents, and safeguard calendar items
Microsoft Purview information protection client	Extending the solution to Windows computers allows users to add labels to File Explorer and PowerShell
Double Key Encryption	Only your organization can decrypt protected content, and you must have the encryption keys in a geographical region
Message encryption	This solution can encrypt email messages and attached files sent to users on any device. This ensures that only authorized individuals can access the contents
Service encryption with customer key	It also complements Microsoft's BitLocker encryption solution to protect data from unauthorized individuals

(continued)

Capability	Type of problem to which solution exists
SharePoint information rights management (IRM)	This solution can also protect libraries and lists in SharePoint so that only authorized individuals can view and use the downloaded files
Rights management connector	It's only suitable for on-premises deployments of Microsoft products, such as Exchange and SharePoint Server, and file servers that run the FCI or Windows Server
Information protection scanner	The solution can discover and protect the sensitive information stored in data stores that are on-site
Microsoft defender for cloud apps	It discovers and protects the sensitive data in cloud-based data stores
Microsoft Purview data map	It applies automatic labeling to the contents of Microsoft Purview data map assets, which include files and databases in Azure Data Lake and Azure Files
Microsoft information protection SDK	Extending the solution to third-party applications and services allows organizations to protect their sensitive content

Prevent Information Loss

These capabilities can be utilized to prevent unauthorized access to sensitive information.

Capability	Type of problem to which solution exists
Microsoft Purview data loss prevention	Avoids accidental sharing of information
Endpoint data loss prevention	This utility enables the extension of data loss prevention (DLP) capabilities to various devices and objects that are used or shared on Windows 10

(*continued*)

Capability	Type of problem to which solution exists
Microsoft Purview extension for Chrome	It extends the capabilities of the DLP feature to the Chrome browser
Microsoft Purview data loss prevention on-premises repositories	This product extends the monitoring and protection of file activities for on-premises and cloud-based data storage. It also provides added security measures for those files in the SharePoint library and folders
Protect sensitive information in Microsoft Teams chat and channel messages	The ability to extend the capabilities of the data loss prevention (DLP) system to include chat and channel messages is a great feature for teams

Govern Your Information

To ensure that you have what you need, and to eliminate what you don't, is essential.

Capability	Type of problem to which solution exists
Retention policies for Microsoft 365 workloads, with retention labels for exceptions	With policy management, you can keep or remove content from emails, documents, and Viva Engage messages
Inactive mailboxes	Mailbox content can be retained after an employee leaves the organization to ensure that it remains accessible for records managers, compliance officers, and administrators
Archive mailboxes	Users can now have more mailbox storage space
Import service for PST files	Exchange Online can now support the import of PST files to keep and search messages for regulatory or compliance purposes

Microsoft Purview Insider Risk Management

Microsoft Purview Insider risk management solution correlates various signals to find potential insider threats, such as data leakage or IP theft. It helps customers create policies to manage their security and compliance. User pseudonyms are used in the design of the solution, and it provides a role-based audit log and access controls that are designed to ensure user privacy.

With the increasing number of employees having access to and sharing data across various platforms and services, organizations are faced with the challenge of identifying and mitigating the risks associated with their data. Unfortunately, most organizations do not have the resources to effectively address these risks. Some of these include the potential theft of data by departing employees and the accidental leaking of information.

The Purview Insider risk management tool from Microsoft provides a comprehensive view of the various indicators that can be used to identify and address potential threats. It can help you quickly identify and take action to minimize the risks associated with our data. Through its log analysis capabilities, you can also define policies that will help prevent unauthorized access and use. Figure 2-5 shows the steps that demonstrate how to configure insider risk management.

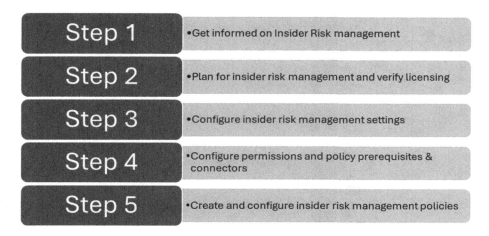

Figure 2-5. Steps to configure insider risk management

Microsoft Purview Privileged Access Management

Being able to maintain standing access to critical network configuration settings or sensitive data in Microsoft Exchange Online can be a potential pathway for internal or external threats. With the help of Microsoft Purview privileged access management solution, organizations can protect themselves from breaches. This solution helps prevent unauthorized access to their data and ensure that they meet the best practices in compliance.

With the help of Purview privileged access management, organizations can implement just-in-time access policies for tasks that require higher privileges. This solution provides a layer of protection against unauthorized access while allowing them to operate with zero privileges. Figure 2-6 display the steps that demonstrate how to configure privileged access management for your organization.

Figure 2-6. *Steps to configure privileged access management for your organization*

Information Governance

Microsoft Purview includes unified data governance solutions that will help you manage data services across your on-premises, multicloud, and software-as-a-service (SaaS) estate that includes Azure Storage services, Power BI, databases like SQL or Hive, and file services like Amazon S3. The solutions included are shown in Figure 2-7.

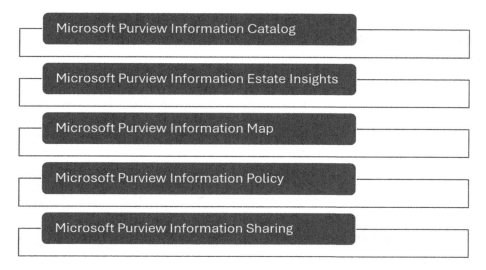

Figure 2-7. *Solution offerings in information governance component*

These tools help organizations create an updated map of their data estate and identify where and how sensitive data is stored. They can also help them manage access to the data in their organization and secure it.

Microsoft Purview Information Catalog

Once data has been ingested into Microsoft Purview data map and is analyzed, consumers need to quickly find the information they need to perform their governance or analytics tasks. This process can be time-consuming since you may not know where to look for the data. Even after you have found the data, you may still have doubts about its trustworthiness.

The goal of searching in Microsoft Purview is make the process of finding the information that matters as fast as possible. This section will teach you how to search the data catalog in Microsoft Purview. Although you don't need specific permissions to search the data catalog, it will only return the most relevant assets that you have access to. Figure 2-8 shows the search user interface UI.

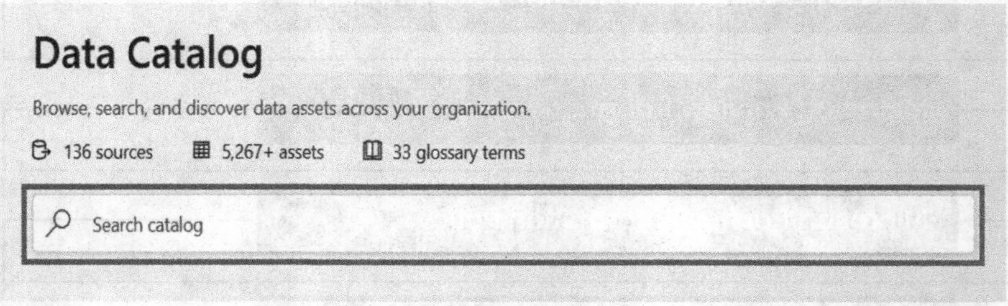

Data Catalog

Browse, search, and discover data assets across your organization.

⟨ 136 sources   ⊞ 5,267+ assets   ▥ 33 glossary terms

🔍 Search catalog

Figure 2-8. *Information or data catalog search use interface*

Microsoft Purview Data Estate Insights

Data Estate Insights is a software that enables governance stakeholders to monitor and manage their organization's data estate. It provides them with insight into the various aspects of their data usage and management. When organizations create their Microsoft Purview data map, Data Estate Insights automatically discovers and highlights governance gaps. This provides drill-down experiences that let data owners and other stakeholders take action to close these gaps.

The reports generated by Data Estate Insights are automatically populated and designed to help governance members focus on the information that they need. The reports and dashboards featured in Data Estate Insights can be categorized into three sections, viz., Health, Inventory and ownership, and Curation and governance, as shown in Figure 2-9.

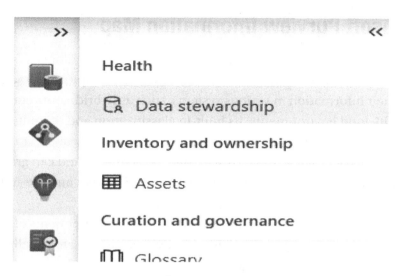

Figure 2-9. *Data Estate Insights categorization*

Health, a good data governance dashboard, can help data managers and quality-focused users identify the current state of their data estate and make informed decisions regarding their investments. It can also help them address any issues that they might have.

Inventory and ownership is focused on summarizing the data estate inventory for users who are mainly focused on data quality and management, such as data curators and stewards. These dashboards provide helpful overviews and metrics to help them identify and resolve various issues related to their assets.

Curation and governance gives an overview of how assets are curated by various curation contexts. Currently, we're focusing on showcasing assets with sensitivity labels, classification, and glossary.

Microsoft Purview Information Map

Microsoft Purview information map is the foundation for information governance and discovery. It enables organizations to capture metadata about their information in various systems, such as hybrid, on-premises, and multicloud environments. Its built-in classification and scanning system help ensure that the map is up to date. The information map for Microsoft Purview accounts starts with one capacity unit and can grow. It can also scale up and down according to the requests sent and the stored metadata.

The operation throughput and metadata storage components of the information map are represented as capacity units, which are usually allocated according to the usage. When a user starts a Purview account, it will automatically start with one capacity unit. It can grow based on the usage. Each unit has a limit of 10 GB of storage and 25 operations per second. The operation throughput is the sum of the various steps involved in creating, reading, writing, updating, and deleting metadata on the Microsoft Purview information map. Some of these include the creation of an asset, adding a relationship to an asset, and editing business metadata. For instance, you can search for a term or description in the asset's metadata and return results.

One of the most common factors that organizations consider when it comes to implementing information governance is the availability of elastic data maps as shown in Figure 2-10. This feature allows them to start with a low-cost data map that can scale up and down according to their usage. This feature can help organizations save money on the initial stages of their data governance projects.

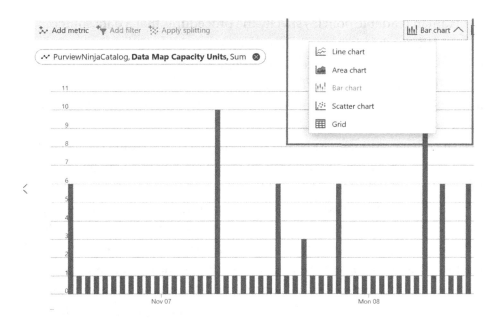

Figure 2-10. *Random visualization of an information map available in Purview*

Microsoft Purview Information Policy

In Microsoft Purview, you can manage the access policies that allow you to access various data systems. For instance, a user needs to access an Azure Storage account in order to perform a computation. You can grant that user this access through the information access policy app, which is available in the governance portal. Only policies that have been enabled for enforcement can be enforced on certain data systems. This can be done through the option turned on in the registration process for data sources.

An information owner policy is a set of policies that describe how a certain entity should treat certain data sources. These policies are then enforced by the other data systems using Microsoft Purview's governance. A policy definition can be used to describe the various policies that are currently in place.

47

Human readable policies specify the procedures that a data source should follow when it comes to handling certain access operations. The four elements of a policy statement are action, effect, resource, and subject.

The operation that is permitted or denied under a policy is referred to as an action. It can be mapped to other actions in the system where it's enforced.

The effect parameter indicates the outcome that should be expected from the data resource and the policy statement if there's a match between the resource and the statement's subject.

A new policy is created in the draft mode during the creation stage, and it can be displayed in Microsoft Purview only. When executed, the policy will be enforced on a specified data system. It can take around 5 minutes to 2 hours for the implementation of this action depending on the type of data source. You can refer to the related policies for guidance on how to implement them.

Policies that are published to a data source may contain statements about a different source. These statements will not be considered since the assets in question are not present in the source where the policy is being enforced.

Microsoft Purview Information Sharing

In the past, organizations typically shared data with external partners and internal teams using a data feed, which resulted in costly investments in data replication and pipeline refresh. This also led to data proliferation and delays in accessing sensitive information.

With the ability to store and share data in place using Azure Data Lake and Azure Storage accounts, organizations can now benefit from the flexibility of having a single view of their data. This eliminates the need for data duplication and enables them to easily manage their sharing activities. Through Microsoft Purview data share, consumers can now gain immediate access to shared data, which is charged based on what they are using. This eliminates the cost of doing business for the data providers.

As shown in Figure 2-11, a data provider can create a share using Microsoft Purview, which is a registration that allows them to select a source and choose which files and folders they want to share. They then send invitations to the consumers. Upon accepting the invitation, the consumer chooses a target storage account that they will use to access their shared data. This type of relationship between the consumer and the data provider allows them to access the shared information in their own storage account. Whenever changes are made to the source account, they are reflected in the consumer's account in real time. The data consumer pays for the privilege of accessing their stored data, while the data provider collects the fees for the privilege of storing their own information. The data provider may revoke the access right at any time, or it can set an expiration date for the privilege. Consumers can also terminate their access at any moment.

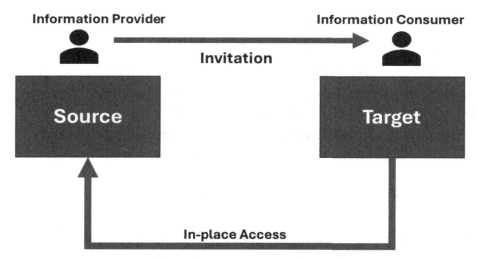

Figure 2-11. *Information sharing in Purview*

Information Compliance

Microsoft Purview includes risk and compliance solutions to help your organization minimize compliance risks and meet regulatory requirements. The solutions described are shown in Figure 2-12.

49

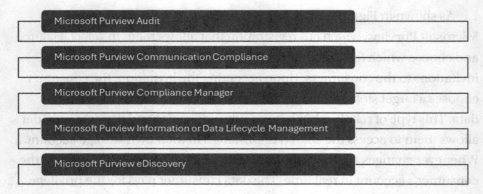

Figure 2-12. *Solution offerings in information governance component*

Microsoft Purview Audit

The Microsoft Purview auditing solution helps organizations address their most critical security and compliance issues. It includes a unified audit log that captures and records every user and admin activity across various Microsoft services and solutions. An audit is a process that allows you to identify and monitor the activities of your organization's security and compliance teams. It can be used to identify areas of weakness and improve the efficiency of your organization. This feature can also help you manage the risk associated with your organization's activities.

Key capabilities available in the Microsoft Purview Audit are Export audit records to CSV file, 180-day audit log retention, thousands of searchable audit events, intelligent insights, and others.

Microsoft Purview Communication Compliance

Communication Compliance from Microsoft helps organizations identify and prevent business conduct violations, such as the sharing of confidential or sensitive information or the harassment of others. It also provides a variety of features that help protect the privacy of its users, such as audit logs and role-based access control.

One of the most critical factors that businesses consider when it comes to meeting their internal standards and policies is the protection of sensitive information. With Microsoft Purview Communication Compliance, they can easily detect and address workplace harassment incidents. It also helps them manage their interactions with Microsoft 365 users. Inappropriate communication may include threatening and harassing messages and actions that share sensitive data within or outside of the organization. The Communication Compliance solution from Microsoft helps organizations detect and address the improper messages that could lead to data security or other compliance issues.

The solution checks the messages sent and received by third-party apps and Microsoft platforms, such as WhatsApp, Teams, Outlook, and Viva Engage. It can also identify potential violations of company policies, such as the distribution of confidential or sensitive information, the harassment of others, and stock manipulation. The goal of Communication Compliance is to help organizations foster secure and compliant communication across their enterprise channels. With role-based authorization, investigators can take action to remove problematic messages from Teams or notify senders of inappropriate conduct.

Communication Compliance from Microsoft provides machine learning tools that can detect messages that may be in violation of an organization's code of conduct or regulatory requirements. Users can configure these tools to identify and evaluate inappropriate messages. The system can also be used to update policy settings according to the needs of the organization. Only the data that is collected and stored by Microsoft is used for internal purposes, and it is not shared with other companies unless explicitly requested by the investigators.

Microsoft Purview Compliance Manager

With Microsoft Purview Compliance Manager, you can easily assess and manage your multicloud environment's compliance requirements. It can help you identify and implement effective controls and manage the various risks associated with data protection.

The Compliance Manager platform provides prebuilt compliance assessments for various industry and regional regulations and standards. It can also help you customize these assessments to meet your specific requirements. Its workflow capabilities can help you complete your risk evaluations more quickly. The suggested improvement actions can be carried out in a step-by-step process to help you meet the regulations and standards that are relevant to your organization. You'll also get a detailed overview of the implementation and audit results of the actions that are being managed by Microsoft. A risk-focused score helps you understand how well you're doing in meeting the requirements.

The overview page of Compliance Manager provides a comprehensive view of your current score and highlights areas for improvement. The points that you're awarded through the improvement actions that are being carried out through Compliance Manager are then combined into an overall score. Each action has an impact on your score, and it can help you prioritize which actions to take to improve your compliance posture. The first score that you receive through Compliance Manager is based on the Microsoft 365 baseline for data protection. This framework includes various regulations and standards related to data protection.

Microsoft Purview Information or Data Lifecycle Management

With the help of Microsoft's data lifecycle management platform, you can easily retain and remove the content that you no longer need. This can be done for various reasons, such as complying with regulatory requirements and ensuring that your data is secure. However, it also helps minimize risk and liability by removing nonbusiness-relevant content.

One of the most important factors that you should consider when it comes to managing your data is the availability of retention policies. These can be used for various Microsoft 365 workloads, such as Exchange, SharePoint, and OneDrive. You can configure the policies to ensure that the content is kept indefinitely or for a specific period.

One of the most flexible options is to automatically remove the content if it isn't already deleted. This can be done through a combination of the two actions, which is very typical. For instance, you can set up a policy that allows you to retain email for three years, then remove it once.

You can also configure the policy to target specific instances within your organization. For instance, you can set it to retain all emails and documents in your organization, or you can set it to only retain those that are specific to one region or department. If you have specific exceptions for certain types of documents or emails, such as those that are legal, you can add a retention label to the content so that it can be automatically applied to apps.

If you're using the solution for insider risk management, then you can use retention labels as part of its adaptive protection. This means that the policy and the auto-apply feature will be automatically generated for you.

Microsoft Purview eDiscovery

The process of eDiscovery involves identifying and delivering information that can be utilized as evidence in a case. You can use tools such as

Microsoft Purview in order to find and retrieve content in various platforms, such as Exchange Online, Office 365, and OneDrive for Business.

In order to search for and extract content from sites and mailboxes, you can use Microsoft Purview eDiscovery standard cases. This tool can also be used to identify and export content found within sites and mailboxes. If you have an Office 365 subscription, then you can use the Microsoft Purview Premium solution to analyze and manage content.

The three different eDiscovery solutions offered by Microsoft Purview are Content search, eDiscovery Standard, and Premium. With the Content search tool, you can easily find and extract content from various sources within Microsoft 365. Microsoft Purview eDiscovery Standard is a follow-up solution to the Content search feature that allows users to create and manage eDiscovery cases. It also lets users associate exports and searches with specific cases.

The eDiscovery Premium tool adds on to the existing capabilities of the standard eDiscovery solution by providing an end-to-end workflow that enables users to analyze, collect, review, and export content. This tool can also be used to identify and extract information from multiple sources. This tool can be used to manage the legal hold notification process and the custodian workflow. It allows users to collect and analyze data from a live service in order to filter and categorize it into review sets. With the help of machine learning and analytics, the eDiscovery Premium tool can be used to further narrow down your search for the most relevant content.

With this, we have come to the end of the chapter and in the chapter, we have seen introduction of Information governance in the Microsoft Purview portal in order to provide a granular approach for Information Governance in a modern enterprise context. Furthermore, we have explored core capabilities of Microsoft purview around information security, information governance, and risk and compliance. In the upcoming chapter, we will be getting into capabilities of the information catalog and metadata management in the Microsoft Purview.

CHAPTER 3

Deep Dive into Information or Data Catalog and Data Management

The goal of Microsoft Purview data catalog is to provide a platform that enables organizations to manage their data and create business value. Data governance has traditionally been a way to ensure that your organization's data is secure. However, good data governance can help organizations keep their data more visible to their users and enable them to connect their data with their business. The new features in the Purview data catalog are designed to make it easier for organizations to manage their data. They are built into a single, integrated software-as-a-service framework. This will allow users to focus on their business instead of switching applications.

In this chapter, we will explore information or data catalog solution of Microsoft Purview with its various data management features such as business domain, data products, data quality, and data access and other features such as data search and data product search, respectively.

© Charles Waghmare 2025
C. Waghmare, *Introducing Microsoft Purview*,
https://doi.org/10.1007/979-8-8688-1204-0_3

Introduction

The rise of AI has created new opportunities for organizations to use and secure their data. Unfortunately, implementing and managing these new tools has been a daunting task. For organizations, managing and securing their data requires both flexibility and rigor. Although it can be hard to maintain consistency across different departments, we believe that a federated approach can help organizations achieve their goals. This type of governance allows them to establish a central repository for data safety and quality, while also providing them with the necessary tools to manage their access. By implementing a federated approach, organizations can greatly benefit from the reduction of bottlenecks and the participation of their various departments in the management and application of their data.

Good data governance is a process that can help organizations improve the efficiency and effectiveness of their operations by ensuring that their data is secure and available. This can be done through the use of a variety of tools and techniques. Having the necessary expertise to manage and secure your data can help minimize the risk of unauthorized access. A good data governance process can also help organizations align their data with their business operations. To access data governance solution in Microsoft Purview, we follow the sequence. Log in to https://purview.microsoft.com/, and we get to home page of Purview as shown in Figure 3-1.

Figure 3-1. *Home page of Microsoft Purview*

Once we enter into the home page of Purview, we can access different solutions such as AI Hub, Compliance Manager, Data Catalog, Data Map, and Information Barriers as shown in Figure 3-2.

Figure 3-2. *Solutions available in Purview*

Once we are into Data Catalog solution home page, as shown in Figure 3-3, we get an opportunity to see different data catalog features such as data search, data product search, data management features, data estate health, and role and permissions section. All of these features will be explained in the upcoming section.

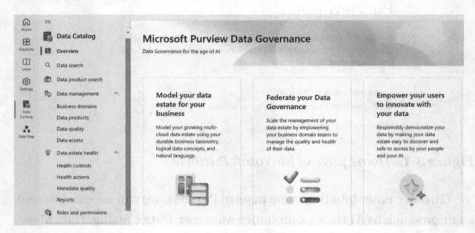

Figure 3-3. *Data Catalog solution home page*

Through the Microsoft Purview data catalog, you can easily explore and understand the various types of data that you have stored and accessed. It includes a variety of tools and resources that allow you to access and manage all of your data assets. We also invested in a powerful platform that allows you to identify and manage all of your data assets. As your data grows, we're providing you with more tools and resources that will help you manage it. These tools will allow you to make informed decisions and improve the efficiency of your business.

Definitions

Before heading into the new section, we will deal with some basic definitions of data governance features which will help us to understand this chapter in a better way, and besides, we will look into details of features in a separate section. We will talk about the various features of the data catalog that support good data governance. We will also explore how these features can help promote the principals of data governance.

- Business domain: It is an organizational object that helps organizations manage their data assets. It provides context and enables easy scaling, for example, customer relationship, external domain, human resources, and operations.

- Access policies: Data catalog access policies provide access to data products in a secure way.

- Critical data element: Describe key business logically to govern them with critical data element.

- Glossary terms: These are active values that are defined as those that provide context while also applying policies that will determine the management and control of your data.

- Data product: It is a kit that includes various data assets such as reports, tables, and files. It provides a convenient way to discover and understand these assets.

- Data estate health: Enable organizations to gain new insights and improve their governance. The health control feature allows you to monitor your governance progress. You can also follow these actions within the data estate to improve the score.

- Data quality: Through the use of AI-powered capabilities, Microsoft Purview data quality can recommend columns for data profiling. This process can help human intervention to improve the accuracy of the recommendations.

Exploring Data Catalog Features

In this section, we will explore all data catalog features with an objective to gain maximum understanding of each feature in order to adopt them with ease and efficiency.

Data Search

When it comes to analyzing and governing data, consumers need to quickly find the information they need to make informed decisions. Unfortunately, finding the data can be time-consuming and challenging due to the lack of knowledge about where to look for it. With Microsoft Purview, users can easily search for the information they need to make informed decisions. The goal of Microsoft Purview search feature as shown in Figure 3-4 is to make it easier to find the data that matters most.

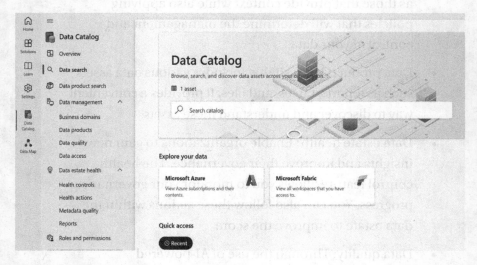

Figure 3-4. Data search feature

You will be notified of your recent searches and the items that were found in the data catalog by selecting the search bar. This lets you quickly retrieve previous searched data "ABC," as shown in Figure 3-5.

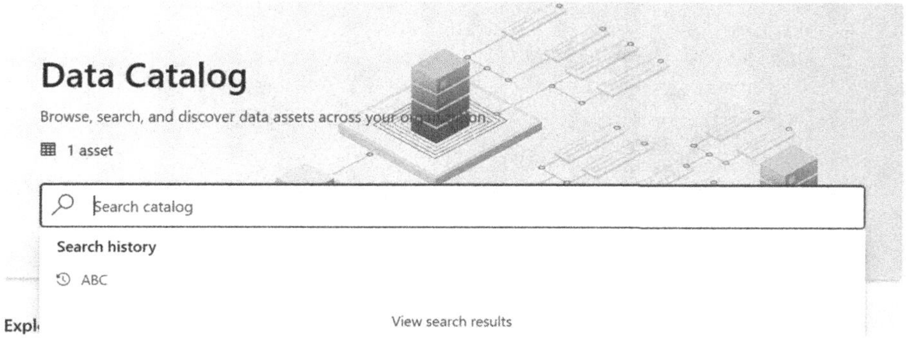

Figure 3-5. *Data Catalog search history*

To narrow down your search results, enter your search query in the form of words that describe your needs, such as data type, name, and classifications. Microsoft Purview will then suggest relevant results and searches that meet your requirements.

Upon entering your search query, Microsoft Purview displays a list of data assets that are associated with your chosen keywords. Users are then tasked with reading the data assets and deciphering the terms. The results will show the exact location of the term that you searched for in the asset. For instance, the term "ABC" was found in the results for the search query.

The relevance score of an asset is computed by the Microsoft Purview search engine based on the various factors that it considers when it comes to assessing the usefulness of a given piece of information. For instance, a data consumer might be more interested in a table that has multiple keywords compared to an uncategorized folder. The company's search team is constantly monitoring the data to ensure that the top results have value to you.

If the search results for your query don't include the items that you're seeking, you can use the filter pane to narrow them down. To do so, go to the left-hand column, and select the category that you want to narrow. Then, select the values that you would like to see in the list as shown in the Figure 3-6.

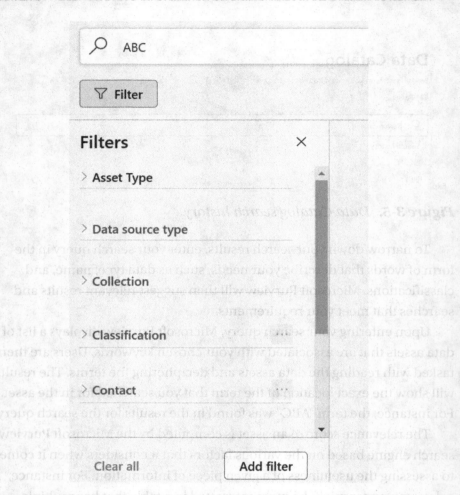

Figure 3-6. Available filters to filter search results

There are multiple filters available. Activity feature allows you to refine your search based on the attributes that were created or updated in a specific period. Asset type feature helps you search for specific types of assets. For instance, you can look for files, metamodels, and dashboards.

Assigned term option helps you search for assets that have the specified terms. Classification option helps you find those that fall under certain categories. Collection feature refines your search for assets in a given collection. Contact option helps you find those that are associated with a specific user.

Data source type option helps you find assets that are from specific sources. For instance, you can search for reports and data stored in Azure Blob storage. Endorsement option helps you search through assets that have specific endorsements, such as promoted or Certified. Label option, on the other hand, helps you search for assets that have specific security labels. Manageable attributes assist in refining your search for assets with specific managed attributes. Listed attributes will be organized using operators, allowing you to look for specific values. Finally, the rating option helps you search for only data assets that have a specific rating. Tags option helps you search for assets with specific tags.

Data Product Search

Having a list of all the available data assets eliminates the need for people to rely on team knowledge and networking skills to find the information they need. However, it can be very hard to keep track of what you're searching for. Having a good overview of all the available data can be very helpful, but it can also be very hard to keep track of what you're actually looking for. Having multiple data assets is also a must for a comprehensive data visualization. As the catalog grows, it needs to be accompanied by a set of contextual tools that will help its users easily access the information they need.

A data product is an organizational concept that consists of a list of associated assets, a name, and descriptions. These assets are grouped together to provide context for consumers. Although a business domain may house multiple data products, they are managed by one entity and can be easily found across different domains. A successful data product allows consumers to easily recognize the value of their data by using their daily language. It also simplifies the ownership responsibilities of these assets.

With data product, a data scientist can create to store all of the assets that they used to create their model. It provides a full use case description and is ideal for anyone who is interested in learning more about how to use the data. As a data product owner, the scientist can now improve the search experience of their consumers by helping them find the information they need. A user can access a data product after they find it and request permission to access all of its associated assets. If there are policies in place for machine learning that allow the use of certain data assets, those policies will automatically apply to the data product.

A data product's access policy is designed to determine how users can access the information they need, the terms of their use, and who should be allowed to access it. These policies can be customizable and will likely evolve over time to cover more use scenarios. All users have to do is select the request access option in the product's interface, and it will automatically send them to the appropriate parties for approval. If you have right access, then you will be able to search data products using below user interface as shown in Figure 3-7.

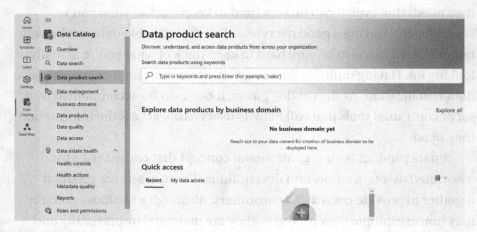

***Figure 3-7.** Data product search interface*

Search results can be filtered based on business domain, data product types, owner, glossary term, and critical data elements as shown in Figure 3-8.

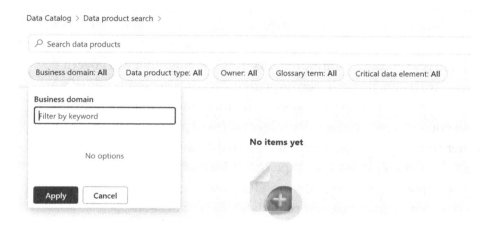

Figure 3-8. *Filtering data product search result*

Data Management

Under data management, there four features, viz., business domain, data products, data quality, and data access.

Business Domain

In Microsoft Purview, a business domain is a new feature that provides a framework for analyzing and managing data assets. It can help organizations make informed decisions and improve their efficiency.

One of the most critical factors that businesses should consider when it comes to implementing a data governance solution is the ownership of their data. Currently, most organizations have a lack of awareness about how to manage their data assets. This is because they don't have a clear understanding of how to discover and maintain their data. The goal of the data catalog was to help businesses establish a connection between their physical and digital data. It was also designed to help them manage their growing data estate more efficiently.

A business domain is an organizational boundary that enables the ownership, management, and exploration of data products and concepts. Its goal is to empower entrepreneurs to create rules that will govern the distribution, use, and access of their data. It is generally focused on various business areas such as sales, finance, and human resources. It also encompasses the broader subject areas of parties, products, and other related entities. A boundary is based on an organization's various functions, such as customer experience, business intelligence, and the cloud supply chain. With Microsoft Purview, organizations can create flexible boundaries that accommodate their data's needs.

Follow these steps to create a new business domain. Go to the Microsoft Purview portal and click the drop-down that will take you to the data management section. Select business domain, and from there, select + New business domain as shown in Figure 3-9.

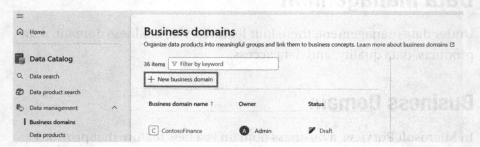

Figure 3-9. *Create a new business domain*

Your business domain should have a unique name and description. The type of business domain that you want to use should be chosen. For instance, you can choose the functional unit, data domain, regulatory project, and line of business. You can also choose an existing domain as the parent one.

Data Products

As defined earlier, it is a kit that includes various data assets such as reports, tables, and files. It provides a convenient way to discover and understand these assets. A data product is an arrangement of information that is organized and designed to be shared with others. An example of this would be a sales report or an ML model. Data products are logical groupings of related physical assets.

Although it can be hard to determine the value of data, it is easier to find it if it is associated with a specific purpose. Having a data product that provides context for your users can help them identify what data they should use. Before you start working on data products, it's important that you have the necessary definitions to make them useful to your users.

To create data products, go to the Microsoft Purview portal and click the drop-down that will take you to the data management section. Select data products, and from there, select + New data products as shown in Figure 3-10.

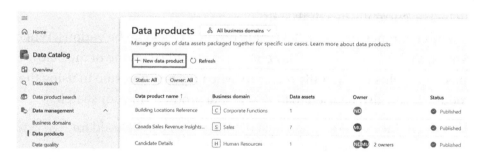

Figure 3-10. *Create new data products*

The basic information such as the name, description, and type should be provided. A business description should describe the data's origins, how it was captured, and what it means to the organization. This type of narrative aims to provide a clear understanding of the data's significance. Then, select Owners for your new data products as shown in Figure 3-11.

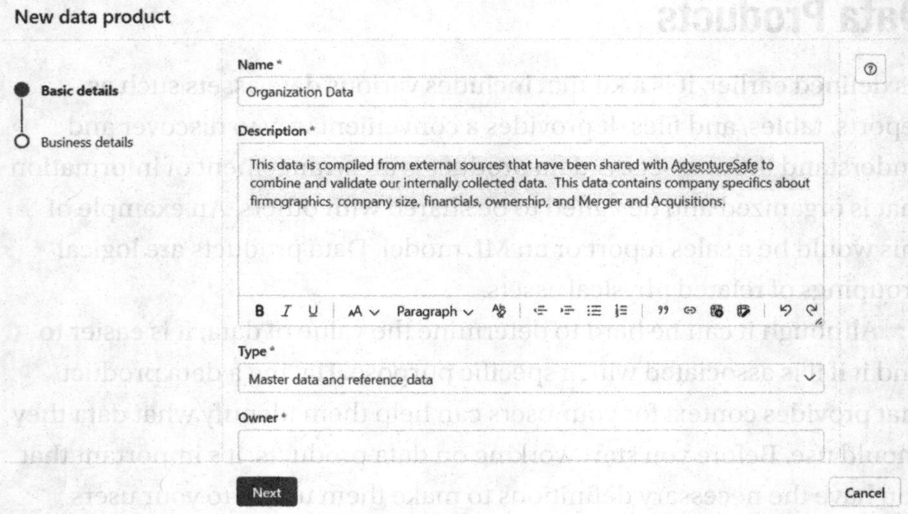

New data product

Name *	
● Basic details	Organization Data
○ Business details	**Description ***
	This data is compiled from external sources that have been shared with AdventureSafe to combine and validate our internally collected data. This data contains company specifics about firmographics, company size, financials, ownership, and Merger and Acquisitions.

B *I* U | AA ∨ Paragraph ∨ A̰ | ⇐ ⇒ ≔ ≔ | ″ ⊖ 🔖 🗍 | ↺ ↻

Type *

Master data and reference data   ∨

Owner *

[Next]   [Cancel]

Figure 3-11. *Description of data products*

Finally, click Next to create a new data product. Upon creating a data product, you are taken to its details page, where you can make changes to it, which is currently in a draft state.

With reference to Figure 3-11, data product types can be various. When creating a data product, you may choose to identify it as one of the below types. This helps you identify the users who may be interested in using the product. It can also be used to filter the data products in your search.

- A **data set** is an analytical data type that can be used for various use cases.

- **Reference and master data** are essential elements that every enterprise should have in its operations, making them the ideal choice for every use case.

- A **business system or application data** is either stored in a single system or in large quantities that can be used to model an entire system.

- The **different types of models are AI, ML, and analytics**. These provide a specific output to be used in developing new applications.

- **Reports and dashboards** are typically used by decision-makers to visualize and analyze data. They help them gain a deeper understanding of the organization.

- The **operational group** is made up of various assets that have to be managed and governed for regulatory purposes.

Data Quality

With Microsoft Purview data quality, data owners and businesses can easily identify and improve the quality of their information ecosystem. This solution helps them ensure that their data is secure and accurate, which is very important in the context of today's AI-driven world.

The lack of data quality can affect a business' decision-making capabilities and processes. With Microsoft Purview data quality, users can easily evaluate the quality of their data by implementing no-code or low-code rules. These rules can be applied across multiple data domains and data assets to provide a comprehensive view of their data quality. Through the use of AI-powered capabilities, Microsoft Purview data quality can also recommend columns for profiling, allowing users to make informed decisions. This process helps improve the accuracy of the data profiling and the overall AI models.

Organizations can enhance, measure, and monitor the quality of their stored data assets through the use of Microsoft Purview data quality. This solution can also help them develop confidence in the use of AI in their decision-making processes and provide them with reliable insights.

Data Quality (DQ) Features

Microsoft Purview offers extensive quality feature for data catalog activities which are shown below:

Data source connection configuration: The configuration of a data source's connection is usually done in steps. The connection should be configured so that the Purview DQ software can access the data for profiling and quality scanning. Managed identity is a type of authentication that MS Purview uses.

Data profiling: The use of AI for data profiling has revolutionized the way organizations collect and analyze information. The standard procedure for analyzing and reporting on industry-standard statistical data is to create a snapshot of the information. To create a comprehensive view of the data, you can drill down into the data and perform data profiling measures.

Data quality rules: The quality dimensions of data are evaluated using six industry standards. These include consistency, uniqueness, completeness, accuracy, conformity, and freshness. The creation features of custom rules include a variety of out-of-the-box functions and expressions. AI integrated rules with auto-generated experience.

Data quality scanning: Assign rules to columns for the data quality scan. Then, apply the data freshness rule in the table or entity level to measure the SLA.

Data quality job monitoring: With the help of this feature, you can monitor the status of data quality jobs and view the history of the scanning process.

Data quality scoring: A data quality score is a measure of how well a rule applied to a given column performs. It can be used to evaluate multiple types of data products and business domains. For instance, one can have multiple data products with different data columns, while another can have multiple data assets.

Data quality for critical data elements (CDEs): One of the most important features of Purview data quality is its ability to create and implement rules that can be used to improve the quality of data collected by CDEs. This allows organizations to establish specific standards and thresholds that they must meet in order to maintain their data quality.

Data quality alerts: With the ability to configure alerts, data owners, and data stewards can be notified whenever the threshold for data quality fails. They can also send notifications to the distribution group or email alias for the affected data.

Data quality actions: The actions center for data quality is where the actions are taken to address the various DQ anomaly states. These include diagnostic queries for the data steward to identify the specific data that needs to be corrected.

Data quality managed virtual network: Private endpoints connected to Azure data sources can be managed through a virtual network maintained by data quality.

By defining data quality features for data cataloging, we will demonstrate their use with few of the DQ features such as data profiling, data scanning, and data quality actions.

Data Profiling: Configure and Execute Data Profiling for a Data Asset
To manage the data quality and data management sections of Microsoft Purview data catalog, go to the menu data management, and click the "data quality" button. Then, select the "business domain" as "Sales" for data profiling as shown in Figure 3-12.

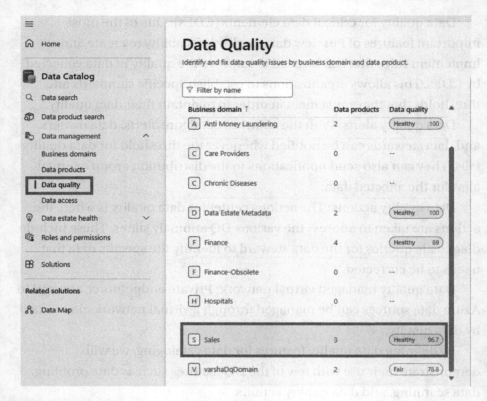

Figure 3-12. *Executing data profiling*

Navigate to the Data quality overview page, and select the data asset you want to analyze as shown in Figure 3-13.

Commercial customers   ×
🏷 Data product

Description
This data product contains commercial customers profile an address data.

Properties

Owner	Business domain	Data quality	Status
(A)(SM) 2 owners	[S] Sales	(Healthy 90)	● published

Data assets

Type: All   Showing 2 item(s)   ▽ Filter by name

Data asset name ↑	Quality score	Asset type
⊞ Customer address	(Healthy 89)	🗄 Azure Data Lake Storage Gen2 Resource Set ⋯
⊞ Customer Profile	(Healthy 91.1)	🗄 Azure Data Lake Storage Gen2 Resource Set ⋯

[OK]   [View detail page]

Figure 3-13. *Analyze a data asset inside Data Quality page*

To perform a profiling job on a specific data asset, select the profile data button as shown in Figure 3-14.

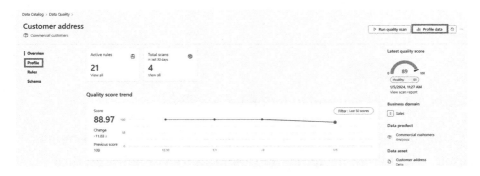

Figure 3-14. *Data profiling for chosen data set*

The AI recommendation engine will show you the most important columns that should be highlighted for profiling. You can also deselect or choose more of them as shown in Figure 3-15, and select run profile.

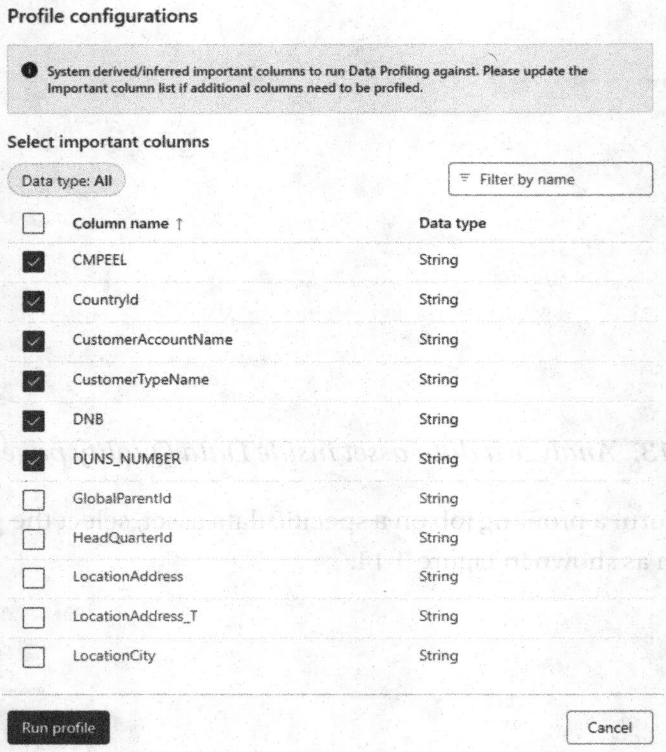

Profile configurations

> ⓘ System derived/inferred important columns to run Data Profiling against. Please update the
> Important column list if additional columns need to be profiled.

Select important columns

Data type: All		⩲ Filter by name

	Column name ↑	Data type
☑	CMPEEL	String
☑	CountryId	String
☑	CustomerAccountName	String
☑	CustomerTypeName	String
☑	DNB	String
☑	DUNS_NUMBER	String
☐	GlobalParentId	String
☐	HeadQuarterId	String
☐	LocationAddress	String
☐	LocationAddress_T	String
☐	LocationCity	String

Run profile   Cancel

Figure 3-15. *AI recommendation for profiling*

After the job is complete, go to the Profile tab and select the "Profile
Result" page to view the results and a statistical snapshot of the data
asset. There might be multiple result pages depending on the number of
columns in the asset as shown in Figure 3-16 with profiling results and
statistical measures for each column.

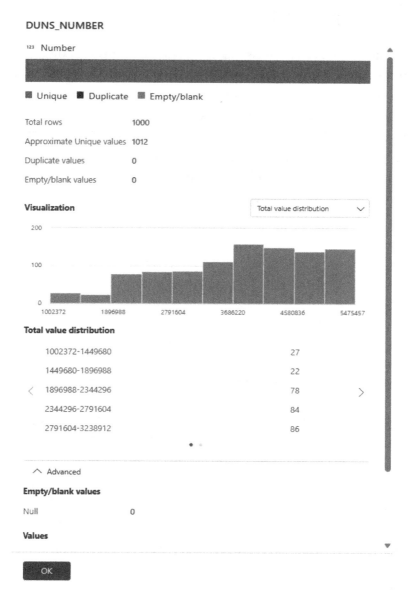

Figure 3-16. *Profiling result summary*

Run a Data Quality Scan

A data quality scan is a process that involves reviewing your data assets and producing a score. This score can be used by your data stewards to identify areas of concern and improve the quality of your data.

If you're not already creating connections to the data sources that you're scanning for quality, you can configure them through the Data management menu in Microsoft Purview data catalog. From the list, select the Business domain that you want to add and choose a domain as "Sales" to assess data quality as shown in Figure 3-17.

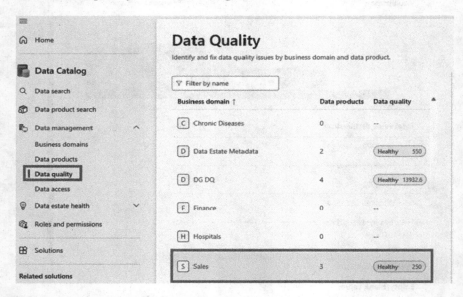

Figure 3-17. *Data Quality scanning*

After choosing domain then, select corresponding data products to assess data quality of data assets linked to this product as shown in Figure 3-18.

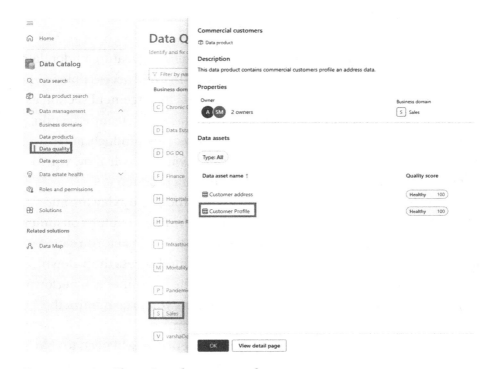

Figure 3-18. *Choosing data assets for assessment*

After hitting the OK button, execute data quality scan as shown in Figure 3-19.

Figure 3-19. *Run data quality scan*

Set Up Data Product Access Policies

Now we have come to the last feature of data cataloging feature under data management. This feature is called data access. To build access policies, go to the Microsoft Purview portal and click the data management section as we have seen in this chapter several times in data catalog feature section, for example, Figure 3-9. From there, you can select the products and manage their policies. The policy configuration window will allow you to create and manage the access policy for your data product.

You can manage the policies for your data products by viewing and editing the default values. These values will determine what the consumers see when they access the request form and how they can act. You can add your own usage conditions under the permitted access drop-down. These will determine the kind of activities that the consumer can perform on the data product. The default values also allow you to customize the description and other features of the request form.

To set up the approval process, select the users who will need to sign on as the first approver. After granting the request, the first approver will then start the process of accessing the data assets. You can also add more approvers by filling out the form with the Microsoft Entra ID or security groups option. Before you start the approval process, make sure that you have the necessary approval and privacy policies in place.

With this, we have come to the end of this chapter. In this journey of the chapter, we have explored information or data catalog solution of Microsoft Purview with its various data management features such as business domain, data products, data quality, and data access and also other features such as data search and data product search, respectively. In the upcoming chapter, we are going to explore another solution of Microsoft Purview called as information discovery and classification.

CHAPTER 4

Information Lifecycle Management and eDiscovery

In the previous chapter, we have discussed an important solution of Microsoft Purview called as information or data catalog and its various data management features such as business domain, data products, data quality, and data access. Further, we have discussed other features such as data search and data product search, respectively. In this chapter, we are going to explore another solution of Microsoft Purview called as Information Compliance where we are going the discuss Information Lifecycle Management and eDiscovery in detail.

Introduction

The Microsoft Purview compliance and risk management solutions help organizations manage their information and comply with regulations. This section provides a comprehensive overview of the various features of these solutions, as well as how they can help you meet your organization's specific compliance needs. The Microsoft Purview suite of compliance and risk management solutions can help organizations comply with regulations and manage their data. These includes Microsoft Purview

© Charles Waghmare 2025
C. Waghmare, *Introducing Microsoft Purview*,
https://doi.org/10.1007/979-8-8688-1204-0_4

Audit, Communication Compliance, Compliance Manager, Information or Data Lifecycle Management, and eDiscovery that exists as shown in Figure 4-1. This solution is also called as risk and compliance solution.

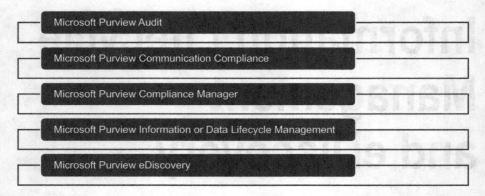

Figure 4-1. *Information Compliance solution in Microsoft Purview*

Before taking deep dive into the specific feature of Information Lifecycle Management and eDiscovery, we will have a quick recap of the all the features of the Information Compliance solution part of Microsoft Purview.

Microsoft Purview Audit

The Microsoft Purview platform provides comprehensive auditing solutions that help organizations respond efficiently to various issues, such as internal investigations and security threats. It also helps them manage their administrative and user operations across multiple Microsoft 365 services. Through the audit records of these events, security, IT, legal, and compliance teams can easily identify areas of their organization that need to be improved. This helps them manage their operations and ensure that they are always focused on the best possible security.

Microsoft Purview Communication Compliance

One of the most important factors that businesses consider when it comes to complying with their internal policies is ensuring that their employees are protected from harassment. With the help of Microsoft Purview Communications Compliance, they can quickly identify and act against inappropriate emails and other communications. This solution can help them prevent these types of threats and ensure that their data is protected.

Microsoft Purview Compliance Manager

With Microsoft Purview records management, an organization can easily manage its legal obligations and ensure that it is following regulations. It can also improve its efficiency by regularly disposing of nonessential items that no longer serve any business purpose.

Microsoft Purview Information or Data Lifecycle Management

With the help of Microsoft's data lifecycle management platform, you can easily retain and remove content across multiple platforms *such as* Exchange, SharePoint, OneDrive, Microsoft 365 Groups, Teams, and Viva Engage. Although it's important to retain and remove messages, emails, and documents for regulatory and compliance reasons, it's also beneficial to delete content that no longer serves any business value.

Microsoft Purview eDiscovery

An eDiscovery process involves identifying and gathering information for a variety of legal and regulatory purposes. Microsoft Purview eDiscovery preview is a tool that lets you search through the content and data in

various Microsoft platforms such as Exchange Online, OneDrive, and
SharePoint. Through the eDiscovery tool, you can search for sites and
mails in the same way. It also lets you export the results for review and
analysis.

Information Lifecycle Management

A data lifecycle management solution helps you manage the end-to-end
process of your organization's content, including all of its physical and
virtual assets, in Microsoft 365. It enables you to automate and secure
the classification and retention of your data, and it provides you with the
necessary insight to make informed decisions.

Use the Microsoft Purview data management and Purview records
management solutions to manage your data for regulatory and compliance
requirements. The following graphic in Figure 4-2 shows the various
configuration options for the Microsoft Purview records management and
data management solutions. These options can be used to manage your
records and comply with various regulations.

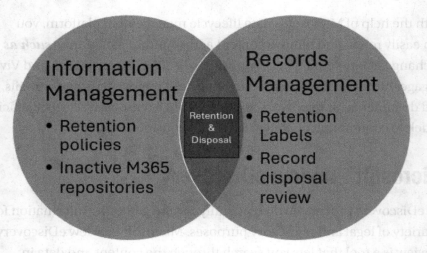

Figure 4-2. Managing information and records in Purview portal

To keep what you need and remove what you don't is the goal. With Information Lifecycle Management, there are capabilities such as Microsoft retention policies, solution for inactive mailboxes and archive mailboxes, and import service for PST files as shown in Figure 4-3.

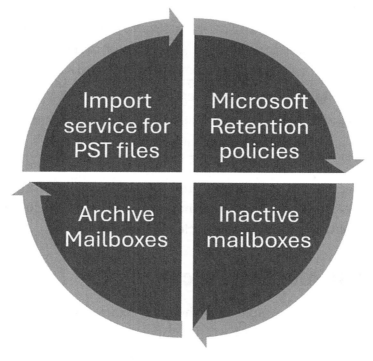

Figure 4-3. *Information Lifecycle Management capabilities*

From Figure 4-3, its capabilities are depicted as below.

Capabilities	Explanation
Microsoft retention policies	Keep or remove content from your email, documents, and Viva Engage messages and across M365 repositories
Inactive mailboxes	Mailbox retention lets you store the contents of your mailbox after an employee leaves the organization. It can then be accessed by records managers, compliance officers, and administrators
Archive mailboxes	Mailbox retention offers users additional storage space
Import service for PST files	Exchange Online mailbox can be used to store and retrieve bulk emails for regulatory or compliance purposes

Data lifecycle management is a process that involves managing the various aspects of a company's information assets. Let's learn more about these capabilities' information lifecycle management space.

Microsoft Retention Policies

Due to the increasing complexity of their data, many organizations are struggling to manage it. This is why it's important that they have the proper tools and resources to effectively manage it. In addition to having the proper tools and resources, it's also important that organizations follow proper internal policies and regulations when it comes to retaining content. For instance, the Sarbanes-Oxley legislation requires companies to retain certain types of data for seven years.

One of the most effective ways to reduce the risk of a security breach or legal action is by permanently deleting all of the old content that's no longer required. Ensure that your users only work with content that's relevant to them and current. This will allow you to share knowledge more effectively. Setting up retention settings can help you achieve these objectives. Two actions are required when managing content.

- Retain: Delete all of your company's eDiscovery content permanently.

- Delete: Keep eDiscovery available and protected from permanent deletion.

You can configure the retention settings to ensure that content is always available for a specific period or forever. Content can be permanently deleted whenever a specified period has passed. Content may be retained for a specific duration and then deleted permanently. These settings allow you to retain your content in place, which eliminates the need for you to create and configure additional storage. You also don't have to implement processes that are customized to sync and copy this data. In this section, various aspects of retention labels and policies are covered. They will help you understand how this work, what they're used for, and how they can complement one another.

Retention settings are used to manage the content in a M365 environment. Content is always in its original location when it is assigned to a retention setting. This ensures that no content changes are made while people continue working on their documents or mail. But if they delete or edit the content that is included in the policy, it is automatically archived. For instance, in OneDrive and SharePoint sites, the copy is archived in the preservation hold library. Copy is also archived in the Recoverable Items section of Exchange mail servers. For teams and individuals using Microsoft 365, the copy is stored in a hidden folder called SubstrateHolds. This is also used in the Recoverable Items section of Exchange. Most people don't see the retention content and secure locations of their websites. In most cases, they don't need to know that they're subject to this type of settings.

In this section, we'll talk about the various types of retention settings that are available for Microsoft products such as OneDrive, SharePoint, and Exchange. We'll also discuss how they can be used to improve the efficiency of your organization.

Retention for SharePoint and OneDrive

OneDrive or SharePoint users can retain all their files by implementing a label or policy. Below types of files can be deleted:

- When retention policy is applied: A retention policy ensures that all files in a document library are preserved.

- When retention label is applied: Only those files with retention label are preserved and others are deleted from the document library.

Although list items do not support retention policies, they can still be supported by retention labels in system lists. This is because these are hidden lists that are used to manage the various components of the SharePoint platform. The labels will retain the list items even if they are not found in the search results.

When attaching a document to a supported item list through a retention label, the attachment doesn't inherit the label's settings; it can still be labeled independently. If the document isn't labeled already, the attachment will automatically inherit the settings of the retention label.

How Retention Works for SharePoint and OneDrive

OneDrive and SharePoint have created a preservation hold library that will automatically retain content if the site doesn't have one. This hidden system location is not designed to be interactive. It only stores files when required for compliance reasons, and it doesn't support the deletion, modification, or movement of these files. You can use tools such as eDiscovery to retrieve these files.

The method utilized by the preservation hold library supports retention labels and policies. Users can modify or delete an item that is subject to a retention policy or label, which indicates that it is a record.

The item's original content is then saved to the library. This method ensures that the original remains available for compliance.

New content is not copied to the preservation hold repository the first time it is edited. To preserve all previous versions, versioning is enabled on the site. When the settings for preserving content were enabled, the behavior of copying files into the repository applies to all content on the site. In addition, content that was created or added after the policy was implemented will be archived in the library.

A timer job is periodically run on the library's preservation hold repository. It compares the content stored in the repository with the queries that were used for the given content. If the content is older than the 30-day retention period, it is deleted from the repository and returned to its original location. The job runs every seven days. With a minimal retention period of 30 days, it takes around 37 days to remove old content from the repository.

If a user tries to remove a list, library, or site that is subject to retention, they will receive an error message. Besides, user may receive an error if they try to remove a labeled item from a list or a library. The item is not replicated to the preservation hold repository but is in its original location. Turning off records management will disable the ability for users to remove labeled items. Items with the retention label are regarded as regulatory records, which means they will never be modified or deleted. Finally, the item's retention label refers to it as a record, and it's locked.

When content is assigned to a SharePoint site or OneDrive account, the path it takes depends on the settings for retention. There are only two options i.e., retain or delete. Modified content is placed in the hold library for policies and labels mark them as records. Items that are modified without labels are placed in hold library and they do not create copies when deleted. When a file is deleted from a document library, it is moved into the first recycle bin and second recycle bin during the 93-day period before it is actually deleted from SharePoint or OneDrive. From the preservation hold library, the file is available for 93 days to retrieve before it is actually deleted from the system as shown in Figure 4-4.

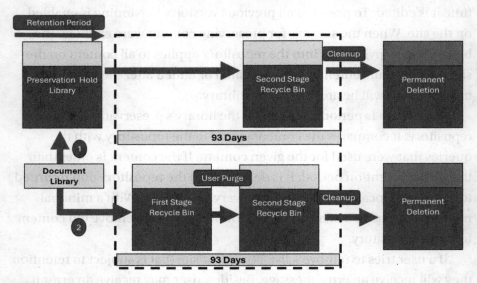

Figure 4-4. *Retention settings are to retain and delete*

With reference to Figure 4-4, if the information is deleted or modified during the retention period and the settings for that were assigned are not used, a copy of that content is created in the library preservation hold. The items that have been moved to the second stage of recycle bin will be permanently deleted at the conclusion of 93 days. Although the second stage recycle bin is not visible to the end users, it can be used by site collection admins to restore and view content.

The content should be moved to the first stage of the recycle bin if it isn't deleted or modified throughout the retention period. Users can either remove or discard the content from this recycle bin, which is referred to as purging, and this item is placed in the second stage. The retention period for documents is generally 93 days. At the end of this period, the content can be permanently deleted from any part of the recycle bin. Because it's not indexed, eDiscovery searches won't be able to find any content in this recycling bin.

For retain-only retention settings, during the retention period, if the content of a document is modified or deleted, it will be stored in the preservation hold library until the end of the period, and it will be deleted after 93 days. The content of a document remains unchanged until the end of the retention period. The original content of the document remains the same as before the retention period. Nothing happens after the period.

For delete-only retention settings, during the specified period, if the content of the document is deleted, it will be transferred to the first stage recycle bin. Users can then either remove the document from this recycle bin or discard it, and it will be placed in the second stage recycle bin. A retention period of 93 days will apply to both the first and second stages. The content of the file will be permanently deleted from its current location after 93 days. If it is modified during this period, it will follow the same path as before.

If the document's content remains unchanged during the specified period, it will be moved to the recycle bin 1 at the end of the policy's retention period. Users can either discard the document or remove it from this recycle bin, which is also referred to as purging, and it will be put in the second stage. The document's content will be permanently deleted from the site where it resides after 93 days, if it has been placed in either the first or second stage recycle bins. Since the recycle bin is not linked to any database, eDiscovery searches can't find the content of the documents in it.

Retention with Cloud Attachments?

Attachments in the cloud are embedded links that users share with or interact with in Microsoft 365. They may be deleted or retained when they are shared in emails or Viva Engage messages or when they are referenced in Copilot conversations. Whenever a user applies a retention label to a cloud attachment, it is applied to a specific copy of the shared file.

For this scenario, the user should configure the start of the retention period to be based on the item's label when it was created. If the user configures the period based on the last modified version, this will take the date from the original file when the item was shared.

If a user changes the original file and then shares it again, a new copy is saved as a new version and labeled in the preservation library hold.

The preservation library hold's labeled date for the original file is updated if it is shared again but no modifications were made. This resets the start of its retention period. Therefore, the start of the hold's retention period should be based on the item label.

As shown in Figure 4-5, the user's retention label doesn't apply to the original file. This prevents it from being modified or deleted by the user. The file is still in the preserve library hold until the job indicates that the period has already expired. If the user chooses to remove items from the list, the file is moved to the second stage of the recycle bin. It will be permanently deleted at the close of 93 days.

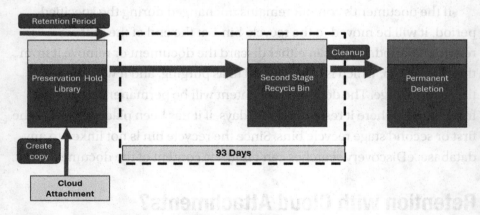

Figure 4-5. *Deletion of cloud attachments*

Following Figure 4-5, the copy saved in the preservation library hold is usually created an hour after the attachment was shared. To prevent the original file from being deleted by users before it can be recreated, files in locations that are included in the policy for auto-labeling are automatically copied to the preservation library hold if they are moved or deleted. These files have a one-day retention period and follow the usual cleanup process.

The original file is retained when it has been moved or deleted, and this version is used when preserving cloud attachments. This feature is unique to the policies for auto-labeling cloud attachments.

Retention with OneNote

As shown in Figure 4-6, when you create a new OneNote folder or place it in a location that includes content from the previous version, the various sections will inherit their settings from the parent section. The pages from these sections will also contain the settings from the new version.

The various sections will be individually deleted and retained according to their respective retention settings. The retention settings that are specified will only affect specific sections. For instance, while you can see a modified date for each notebook, it is not used for Microsoft 365 retention.

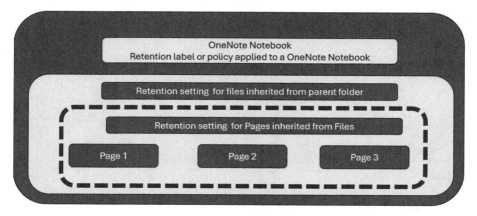

Figure 4-6. *Retention with OneNote*

Note   The preservation hold library keeps separate versions of each record, which makes them potentially expire independently of the current one.

Whenever a user leaves a company, their content will not be affected by the changes in the collaborative environment of SharePoint. This is because it is a different environment from a user's account in OneDrive or Mailbox. If a user leaves a company, their content will not be affected by the changes in the collaborative environment of SharePoint. The settings for the retention period will remain the same as they were when they were first created. Even after the user has left, all of their shared files will still be accessible through the content search and eDiscovery tools. After the retention period has ended, the content will be moved to the site collection recycle bin and inaccessible to everyone except the admin.

The configuration can be done through either the Microsoft Purviews portal or the Microsoft compliance portal. To configure the retention policies, go to the Microsoft Purview portal's solutions section. To start the configuration process, select the new retention policy option and then name it as shown in Figure 4-7.

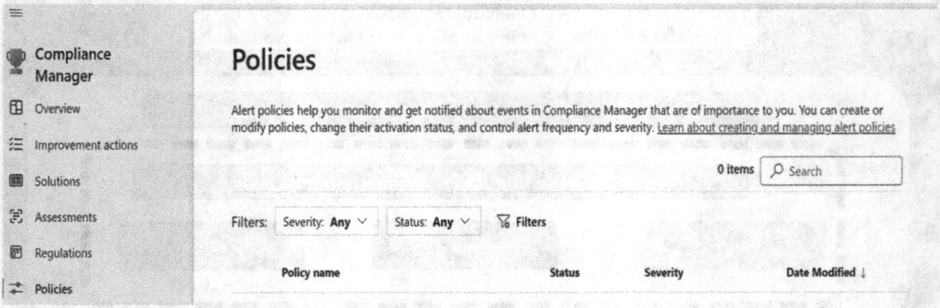

Figure 4-7. Configuration of policies

Retention for Microsoft Teams

A retention policy can be used to retain the data collected from chats and messages in Teams. It can also be used to delete these messages and actions. In order to store the data, it is stored in Exchange mailboxes. Chats data is placed in a hidden folder inside the inbox of each user, while channel messages are stored in a similar folder in a group mailbox. Although these folders aren't directly accessible to administrators or users, they can be used to store important data that compliance officials can access through eDiscovery tools. The attributes of these mailboxes are listed below in the Recipient Details section of the Exchange app.

- The UserMailbox is a type of mailbox that stores messages for users on private channels and those using the cloud-based version of Teams.

- The MailUser is a type of mailbox that stores messages sent to on-premises users of Teams.

- The group mailbox is used to store messages sent to standard channels in Teams.

- The SubstrateGroup mailbox holds messages sent to Teams' shared channels.

Messages and chat logs from Teams in Exchange Online are stored in the SubstrateHolds folder, and permanent deletion from this folder is suspended whenever a different policy is applied to the same mailbox. This can be due to a delay hold, eDiscovery hold, or litigation hold. Messages and chat logs that have been deleted from the team app will not be visible in the Teams app, but they can still be discovered through eDiscovery.

When a channel and chat policy is set up, the path to the content of the messages and chat logs will depend on whether the retention policy is to retain and then delete, to retain only, or delete only as shown in Figure 4-8.

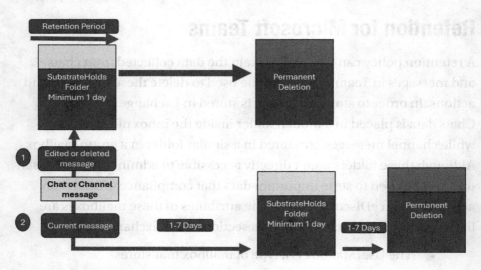

Figure 4-8. *Retention in Microsoft Teams*

From above Figure 4-8, a user can either copy or remove a channel or chat message during the retention period. If the original message is deleted, it is moved to the SubstrateHolds folder, while if it is edited, it is copied. Even though the message is no longer in the Teams app, it remains in the repository for 21 days. Messages are stored in the SubstrateHolds folder for a maximum of one day. If the policy is set to retain forever, it will automatically remove the item when the timer job ends. On the other hand, if the policy has an expiration date, it will permanently delete the message once it runs out. Messages that are not edited or deleted by a user during the retention period will remain in their original location. Also, nothing happens after the period has ended.

Following Figure 4-8, during the retention period, a user can either copy or delete a channel or chat message. If the user deletes a message from the Teams app, it doesn't go into the Folders section of the SubstrateHolds app. However, it remains in the system for up to 21 days after it is removed. The message is then permanently deleted once the timer job has run. Messages that remain after the retention period are transferred to the SubstrateHolds folder at the end of it. This process lasts for up to 1 day, and it permanently deletes them the next time a timer job is run.

Retention for Viva Engage

Viva Engage messages are stored in Exchange Online mailboxes. In case the messages are affected by another policy, such as litigation hold, eDiscovery hold, or delay hold, the permanent deletion from SubstrateHolds is suspended. Although the messages in the Viva Engage feature are included in an eDiscovery hold, they will still be accessible through the eDiscovery process.

As shown in Figure 4-9, when a Viva Engage retention policy is set up, the messages' paths are affected by the option to retain or delete.

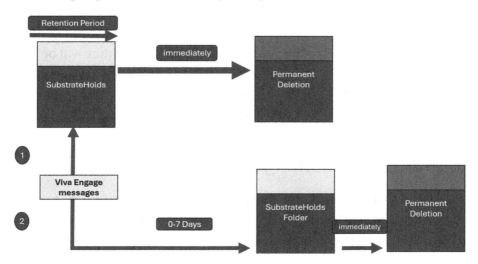

Figure 4-9. *Retention in Viva Engage*

As shown in Figure 4-9, with number 1, the original message of Viva Engage is automatically copied and moved to the SubstrateHolds folder if it is deleted or edited by the user. The message is then permanently deleted once the retention period has ended.

Also, as shown in Figure 4-9 with number 2, if a message from Viva Engage is not deleted after editing, it will be moved to the SubstrateHolds folder, and it will be permanently deleted once the retention period ends. This happens within seven days from the date of the message's expiration.

In a case of retention-only policy, if a Viva Engage message is deleted or edited, a copy of it will be created in the SubstrateHolds folder and kept there until its retention period has ended. The message will then be deleted permanently. The Viva Engage message can be deleted or modified, but it will remain in its original location. If it is not modified, nothing happens after the retention period.

In case of delete-only policy, messages from Viva Engage may not be deleted if they remain in the retention period. After the period has ended, the messages are placed in the SubstrateHolds folder, and they will be permanently deleted once the expiration date has passed. If a user deletes the Viva Engage message during the period, it will be transferred to the SubstrateHolds folder, which will permanently delete it.

Retention for Exchange

Folders and mailboxes utilize the Recoverable Items repository to store items. Only those with eDiscovery permissions can access it. When a user creates a new folder and deletes a message from it other than the one in the deleted items folder, the message is placed in the deleted items. However, users can also soft delete items in other folders and move them to the Recoverable Items repository.

When a user applies a retention policy to Exchange data, an automatic timer job will periodically check the items in the Recoverable Items folder for any discrepancies. If the item doesn't meet the requirements of a retention label or policy, it is permanently deleted. Also, if the item is configured for a disposition review, it is not deleted from the repository until the confirmation is received.

As shown in Figure 4-10, when implementing Exchange content retention policies, the paths that the content takes are dependent on the settings. For instance, if the policy is to retain only, then the content will take a different path. When retention setting is to retain and delete then path is different. Both paths are shown in Figure 4-10.

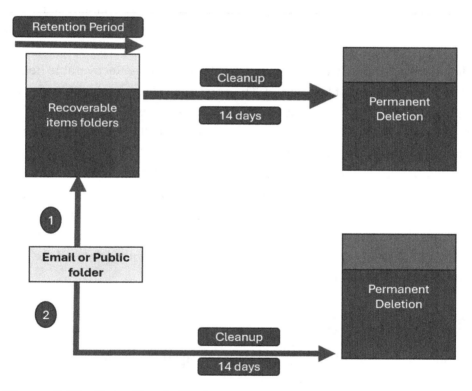

Figure 4-10. *Retention in Exchange*

As per Figure 4-10 number 1, user can permanently or modify an item by deleting it or adding it to the list. This method works by moving it to the Recoverable Items folder, where it will be archived along with the other items that have been previously deleted. Once the retention period has ended, a timer job will automatically identify and delete the items that have been previously modified. The default setting for this is 14 days, but this can be changed to 30 days.

As per Figure 4-10 number 2, the process will automatically update the status of the selected item every 10 days if it's not modified or deleted within the retention period. The items that have been identified as having expired will be deleted from the mailbox within 14 days of the expiration of the period. The default setting is 14 days, but it can be changed to up to 30 days.

For retain-only settings, during the retention period, if an item is deleted or modified, a copy of the original is kept in the Recoverable Items folder until the end of this period. The copy that was created within the folder is deleted within 14 days following the item's expiration. If the item is still intact during the retention period, nothing will happen prior to or after the period. The item stays in its original place.

For delete-only settings, in case the item isn't deleted during the retention policy's period, it will be moved to the Recoverable Items folder. If an item is deleted during the specified period, it will be placed in the Recoverable Items category. Users can either remove it from the repository or put it in the recycle folders, and it will be permanently deleted if they do so, or the item has been in the category for 14 days.

Retention for Copilot

When a Microsoft 365 retention policy is set up, the path to content creation and deletion considers the option to retain or only retain.

Following Figure 4-11 number 1, messages that are removed from Copilot are stored in the SubstrateHolds folder. They will remain there for one day. Whenever the retention period ends, the message is deleted the next time a timer job is completed.

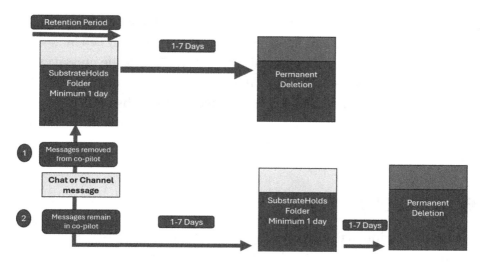

Figure 4-11. *Retention in Copilot*

Following Figure 4-11 number 2, messages that remain in Copilot following the expiration of the retention period will be stored in SubstrateHold's folder. This process typically takes around 1-7 days. Once the message has been placed in the folder, it will remain there for at least one day before it is deleted once a timer job finishes.

After the retention period ends, messages that remain in Copilot will be stored in the SubstrateHolds folder. They will then be deleted the next time a job is completed. The reason why these messages appear in the app again after a short period of time is due to the delays in the communication between the backend service and the user app.

For retain-only retention policy, messages that have been removed from Copilot are placed in the SubstrateHolds folder once the retention period has ended. This process can take up to 7 days. If the policy is configured to automatically retain the item, it will remain there until the end of the period. On the other hand, if the policy has an expiration date, the message will be deleted once more. Messages that remain in the Copilot system after the retention period has ended will remain in their original location. Nothing will happen after that period.

For delete-only retention policy, messages that were removed from Copilot are stored in a SubstrateHolds folder, and they can be retrieved only once the timer job has run. For 1 to 7 days, the messages are permanently deleted. Messages that were left in Copilot after the expiration of the retention period are archived in the SubstrateHolds directory. This process can take up to 7 days, and it permanently deletes them once the timer job has finished.

eDiscovery

In this last section of this chapter, we will discuss about eDiscovery solution part of Microsoft Purview. Microsoft Purview provides three eDiscovery solutions: Content search, eDiscovery (Standard), and eDiscovery (Premium).

The Content search tool can find and extract content from various sources within Microsoft 365. It can also export results to a local computer.

The Standard version of eDiscovery adds a variety of features to the content search tool, such as creating and managing eDiscovery cases. It allows you to assign eDiscovery managers specific cases and lets you associate searches with specific cases.

The eDiscovery Premium version of software adds a variety of features to the eDiscovery workflow, such as the ability to collect, analyze, and export content. It also provides an end-to-end view of the content. The legal hold notification workflow allows teams to communicate with the involved custodians. It also lets you collect and copy data from live services into review sets. With the ability to filter, search, and categorize content, it helps you find and prioritize the most relevant information. The eDiscovery Premium version of software includes machine learning and analytics capabilities. These tools can help you narrow down your search and find the most relevant information.

Capabilities of eDiscovery

Below is the list of capabilities of eDiscovery under Purview.

- Search for content: You can search for the content of various Microsoft 365 applications, such as Exchange, OneDrive for Business, and SharePoint sites. You can also look for content generated by other apps that store data in sites and mailboxes.

- Keyword queries and search conditions: Creating and implementing keyword query language (KQL) queries is useful when you're looking for specific content terms that match your query criteria. You may also want to narrow your search by adding conditions.

- Search statistics: You can view the statistics of your search results after you run a search. These include the total number of items that match your query's criteria and the size of each item. You can also see which content locations contain the most results.

- Case management: In eDiscovery cases, you can associate specific searches with an investigation. With the ability to assign members to a case, you can also control who can access it and view its contents. This feature is useful when you're working on a case that's related to Microsoft Purview Insider risk management solution.

- Place content locations on legal hold: When preserving important information during an eDiscovery investigation, you can place a legal hold on certain content locations. This ensures that sensitive data is protected from accidental deletion or intentional destruction.

- Legal hold notifications: You can manage the communication between case custodians and your legal hold notifications. You can keep track of the notices that were sent, read, or acknowledged by the individuals who are responsible for preserving the content. With the ability for creating and sending escalations and notifications, the eDiscovery Premium platform can help you keep track of the status of your hold.

- Error remediation: In order to fix eDiscovery Premium's processing errors, you can perform a process known as error remediation. This allows you to identify and fix the issues that prevent the company from properly processing your content. For instance, if you're trying to process files that are encrypted or locked, you might end up with a 404 error message. You can then download the affected files and manually upload them to the eDiscovery platform.

- Optical character recognition (OCR): When a review set is added to, eDiscovery Premium's OCR feature extracts the text from the images and includes the associated image text in the review set. This feature is useful when you're looking for specific image text.

- Conversation threading: When a chat message from Viva Engage and Teams is included in a review set, it can be collected as part of the conversation thread. This feature lets you review the items in the exchange based on the collection criteria.

- Collection statistics and reports: After creating a collection estimate or starting a review set, eDiscovery Premium provides a variety of reports and statistics about the items that were collected. These include the number of items that were returned by a search query, the content locations that had the most matching items, and the overall collection statistics.

- Analytics: eDiscovery Premium's analytics tools can help you analyze the documents in a way that's more efficient and reduce the amount of time that you spend reviewing them. One of the most useful features of this tool is the ability to identify near duplicates in the review set. This feature can help you save time and effort by finding similar documents. The email threading feature can help you contextualize the conversations in an email thread by identifying specific messages. In addition, the themes functionality can help you analyze the related themes in the review set and assign one to the documents so that you can easily review them. These capabilities can help make the review process more efficient, allowing you to get a fraction of the documents that were collected.

- Predictive coding models: With the help of predictive coding models, you can reduce the amount of case content that you have to review by identifying the most relevant items in the review set. This process can be achieved through the training of the models and the implementation of prediction scores on the various items in the review set.

With this, we have come to the end of this chapter. In this chapter, we have explored another feature of Microsoft Purview called as Information Compliance with its features such as Microsoft Purview Audit, Communication Compliance, Compliance Manager, Information or Data Lifecycle Management, and eDiscovery. Out of these, we have explored Information or Data Lifecycle Management and eDiscovery in detail. In the next chapter, we will provide a ground level approach for data lineage and mapping using Microsoft Purview.

CHAPTER 5

Data Lineage and Mapping

In the previous chapter, we have explored Information Compliance and its features such as Microsoft Purview Audit, Communication Compliance, Compliance Manager, Information or Data Lifecycle Management, and eDiscovery. Out of these, we have explored Information or Data Lifecycle Management and eDiscovery in detail. In this chapter, we are going to cover data lineage and data mapping features of data governance solution of Microsoft Purview. We will be covering introductions, understandings, features, benefits, practical applications, implementation, challenges, and considerations of data lineage and data mapping, respectively.

Introduction

Understanding the various steps involved in the transformation and movement of data is very important in order to make informed decisions and improve the efficiency of your organization. Data lineage is a process that helps you identify the path that data goes through. It provides a detailed map of the data's journey. A data lineage process helps organizations maintain the quality and accuracy of their data by providing insight into its transformations and flow. It is an essential part of data governance, which supports regulatory compliance and transparency.

© Charles Waghmare 2025
C. Waghmare, *Introducing Microsoft Purview*,
https://doi.org/10.1007/979-8-8688-1204-0_5

Data lineage is a critical component of Microsoft Purview. It serves various important functions. The data lineage visualization helps visualize the various processes and systems that move data from one place to another. It also shows how data undergoes transformations. One of the most important functions of data lineage is to track the transformations that happen in the data. This process helps ensure that the data is accurate and consistent. It helps organizations identify and resolve data quality issues by visualizing the transformations and flow of information. Data lineage also helps in identifying where inconsistencies or errors originate and how they can be propagated through the system. Providing a clear audit trail for transformations and movements ensures compliance with regulations such as HIPAA, GDPR, and CCPA. This is important for organizations. Through data lineage, organizations can easily understand the impact of changes on their data sources and processes. It helps them identify how these modifications might affect their consumers and the downstream operations as shown in Figure 5-1.

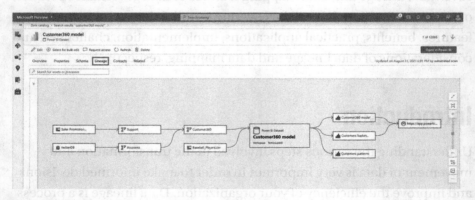

Figure 5-1. *Data lineage diagram impact of changes in data sources and processes. affecting consumers and the downstream operations*

Features of Data Lineage

The Microsoft Purview data lineage suite includes features designed to improve the management and governance of information as follows:

- The end-to-end lineage feature of Purview allows organizations to track the flow of information from its source to its destination. It includes the various stages of the data's journey, such as transformations and processing.

- Users can explore and understand the various aspects of data lineage through interactive visualizations. These tools provide a visual representation of the transformations and data flow, allowing them to identify specific dependencies and processes.

- Microsoft Purview can automate the discovery of lineage information across various systems and sources. This feature helps organizations reduce the manual work involved in mapping lineages and ensure that the information is up-to-date.

- The integration of Purview with other sources, such as data lakes and cloud platforms, ensures that lineage tracking can be carried out seamlessly across different environments.

- The ability to track the data lineage through detailed audits is a vital part of Purview's platform for ensuring that organizations follow proper regulations.

- Through impact analysis, users can learn about the possible effects of changes to processes or data sources. This capability is useful when it comes to ensuring data quality and managing risks.

Benefits of Data Lineage in Microsoft Purview

Implementing a data lineage solution through Microsoft Purview can provide organizations with numerous advantages as follows:

- A data lineage solution provides a detailed view of how information is transported and transformed across an organization's various systems. This transparency allows users to gain a deeper understanding of how data is organized and used.

- By monitoring and visualizing the transformations of data, organizations can identify issues that may affect its quality. This helps them make better decisions and improve the accuracy of their data.

- A data lineage solution can help with efficient troubleshooting by providing insight into how and where issues originated. This can speed up the resolution of such problems and minimize disruptions.

- Data lineage can also help with regulatory compliance, as it provides an audit trail of how information is being transported and transformed. This is important for ensuring that the organization is following legal requirements.

- By understanding the data lineage, an organization can improve its decision-making process by gaining a deeper understanding of how information is being collected, transported, and transformed. This can help boost business outcomes and ensure that data is reliable and accurate.

- A data lineage is an essential part of data governance, as it enables organizations to manage and control their information assets. It also supports various practices related to data management and stewardship.

How Data Lineage Works in Microsoft Purview

In Microsoft Purview, data lineage is a process that involves multiple steps. There are many steps involved in the process.

- Through the integration of Purview with various data sources, such as cloud platforms and databases, it can access and track data from different environments and systems.

- In order to find data lineage, Purview uses a combination of manual and automated methods. The latter involves analyzing various sources and processing them to identify transformations and flows. Manual methods can also include user configuration and input.

- Upon discovering data lineage, Purview maps the transformations and flow processes, providing a comprehensive view of how information moves across the system. This feature also serves as a visual representation of the destinations, sources, and transformations.

- With the ability to visualize data lineage, Purview allows users to gain a deeper understanding of how information flows across the system. It can customize the visualizations and provide a clear view of how data is moving.

- The information about data lineage is continuously updated as the processes and sources change. With Purview, users can keep track of any changes in the environment and ensure that the lineage data is accurate.

Use Cases for Data Lineage in Microsoft Purview

Microsoft Purview can be used to implement data lineage in various scenarios and industries:

- Through data lineage, organizations can improve the quality of their data by identifying and resolving issues related to its processing and transformations. This ensures that their data stays reliable and accurate.

- By having a clear understanding of the movement and transformations of their data, organizations can comply with various regulations such as the Health Insurance Portability and Accountability Act of 1996 (HIPAA), the General Data Protection Regulation (GDPR), and the Credit Card Processing Act of 2012. This capability helps them avoid potential legal issues.

- Data lineage can also be used to manage the effects of changes on various processes and sources. This helps prevent the effects of these changes from negatively affecting the operations of the business.

- Through data lineage, organizations can also identify and resolve data-related issues by gaining a deeper understanding of their sources and how they originated. This helps in reducing the chances of disruptions and improving the quality of their data.

- The data lineage feature of Purview provides comprehensive visibility into the usage, transformations, and assets of data. It enhances data management techniques and helps in the effective management of information.

Integration with Other Microsoft Purview Features

Microsoft Purview's data lineage feature is integrated with other capabilities of the platform, making it more valuable.

- Through the data catalog, users can easily access lineage information, which is associated with the main data assets in Purview. This feature helps them discover and contextualize their data.

- Through the integration of the data classification and lineage features, users can gain deeper insight into the classification of their data. This allows them to ensure that it is properly handled.

- The data lineage feature delivers a comprehensive view of the quality and usage of your data. It helps users improve their data management and generate actionable insights.

- The ability to store and manage lineage information helps organizations comply with regulations. It also enables them to meet their risk management and data governance goals.

Challenges and Considerations

Although data lineage in Microsoft Windows Purview provides numerous advantages, it should be noted that organizations should also be aware of the various considerations that come with it.

- In complex data environments, it can be challenging to accurately capture and visualize the data lineage. To effectively manage these scenarios, organizations should invest in additional tools and resources.

- In order to avoid unauthorized access and disclosure of sensitive information, organizations must implement suitable access and security controls.

- Maintaining the information lineage continuously requires an ongoing effort, as processes and sources change over time. This is why it is important that organizations have procedures in place that regularly update and maintain the information.

- Implementing a data lineage solution with a legacy system or non-standard sources can be a bit challenging. To ensure that the integration goes well, organizations should prepare for possible scenarios and allocate resources for the necessary steps.

Best Practices for Implementing Data Lineage in Microsoft Purview

Best practices are necessary to ensure that organizations can benefit from the data lineage capabilities of Microsoft Purview.

- Before implementing Microsoft Purview, it is important that the requirements and objectives of the data lineage are clearly defined. This will help guide the process and ensure that the information collected meets the needs of the organization.

- Using Purview's automated discovery capabilities can help organizations reduce the manual effort involved in their data lineage management. It can also help them ensure that the information is updated and accurate.

- Integrating the data lineage with other systems and sources can provide an in-depth view of how information is being moved and transformed. This approach can help organizations establish a comprehensive data governance and management strategy.

- Establishing procedures for maintaining and updating data lineage information can help ensure that the details stay current and reflect changes in the organization's data environment.

- To ensure that their sensitive information is protected, organizations should implement proper access and security controls. This is important for maintaining regulatory compliance and data privacy.

- People should be trained on how to take advantage of the data lineage's features. This can help them make better decisions and improve data management techniques.

Microsoft Purview's data lineage feature helps organizations improve the quality and transparency of their data. It enables them to manage their data assets more effectively and comply with regulations. The integration of other features such as data discovery and classification help boost the value of this feature. As organizations continue to expand their data operations, the need for data lineage will become more critical. Its ability to improve the quality and transparency of their data is a vital part of any organization's strategy to manage its data assets. Despite the challenges that it faces, data lineage is still a powerful tool that can help organizations achieve their goals. Using Purview's advanced lineage capabilities and following best practices can help organizations make informed decisions, keep track of their data's quality, and comply with regulations. This can result in improved business outcomes and regulatory compliance.

Data Lineage Examples in Microsoft Purview

In Microsoft Purview, the data lineage view provides a comprehensive view of how information moves across various systems. Understanding the various steps involved in the data's journey is very important in ensuring that it is processed and maintained properly. We'll explore several scenarios that demonstrate how this feature can be used in different applications.

Example 1: A Data Pipeline Is Created in a Cloud-Based Data Warehouse. It Shows How Information Moves Across Different Systems

A large retailer uses a data warehouse, such Azure Synapse Analytics, for gathering and analyzing sales data. Before it can be used for reporting and business intelligence, the company wants to know how the data is processed.

- The process begins with the ingestion of data from various sources, such as third-party sales platforms and point-of-sale systems. Microsoft Purview then automatically captures the data lineage as it is processed and ingested into the warehouse.

- After data is ingested, various transformations are performed, such as data cleansing, enrichment, and aggregation. For instance, sales data can be aggregated by product categories and regions. These transformations are then tracked and updated through the data lineage.

- The processed data is then stored in various views and tables within the data warehouse. With Purview, you can see how the transformed information is organized and where it is stored.

- The stored and transformed data is then fed into business intelligence tools, which can then be used to analyze and report on the information.

The ability to visualize the entire data lineage is a powerful feature in Microsoft Purview. It allows organizations to understand how their data is processed and maintained.

Example 2: The Second Example Deals with the End-to-End Process Involved in Regulatory Compliance

In order to comply with the GDPR, a financial services firm must regularly monitor and audit how sensitive customer information is being distributed across its systems.

- The process of gathering customer information involves various channels. This includes third-party providers, online forms, and customer service interactions. As it flows into the organization's systems, Purview captures the connection between this data and its lineage.

- The information collected is then processed in various steps, such as validating the data and assessing its risk. This process can involve validating the data against external databases or adding credit scores or other personal information.

- The gathered customer information is encrypted in a secure database. With Purview, organizations can monitor and analyze how this information is being stored, as well as its location and access history. It also keeps track of who has access to this information and how it is utilized.

- The company must also generate reports about the activities related to the processing and access of its data. With the help of Purview's lineage capabilities, it can provide a comprehensive view of the data's movement and changes, helping it meet the GDPR's requirements.

In this scenario, it is essential that the company has the proper data lineage capabilities to ensure regulatory compliance and accurate records of its processing activities.

Example 3: Data Lineage for a Marketing Campaign

A consumer goods company operates marketing campaigns across various channels, including digital adverts, social media, and email. Through Microsoft Purview, they can monitor the flow of marketing data as it is collected, analyzed, and reported.

- The company's marketing data is gathered from various sources, such as social media interactions, email open rates, and ad performance. With Microsoft Purview, it can then be analyzed and reported.

- Through the aggregation and transformation of data, the company can gain a deeper understanding of its marketing campaigns. For instance, by combining data from different channels, it can create a more comprehensive view of its effectiveness.

- Data analysts use the collected information to generate recommendations and insights for future campaigns. With Microsoft Purview, they can also see how the data is being used and the sources of information that are used in reports.

- The data analysis process leads to the creation of reports and dashboards, which serve as a guide for decision-making and marketing strategy. Purview also keeps track of the sources of information used in the reports.

Purview's data lineage capabilities can help organizations determine the flow of marketing information and ensure that their decisions are based on precise data.

Example of Lineage from Power BI into Microsoft Purview

Upon a Power BI source's scan, lineage information for all of your data assets will automatically be added to Microsoft Purview's Data catalog. Data consumers can also perform root cause analysis to identify any discrepancies in a report or dashboard. Through the Power BI source's downstream reports and dashboards, data producers can easily see how their data is being used. Before making changes to their data, they can also make informed decisions. In addition, users can search for relevant artifacts by name, owner, sensitivity label, and other business aspects.

After you have completed the Power BI scan, the following artifacts will be made available in Microsoft Purview. These include Sales health reports, dashboards, dataflows, data sets, and workspaces as shown in Figure 5-2.

Figure 5-2. *Power BI scan*

The Power BI artifact search feature allows users to look for relevant results by searching for details such as the name, description, and classification of the asset. The properties and overview tabs show the basic information about the asset, such as its classification. The lineage tab displays the relationships between the upstream and downstream pipelines.

Through Microsoft Purview, users can identify the lineage of their Power BI artifacts (e.g., dataflow ➤ data set ➤ report ➤ dashboard). For instance, they can look for connections between the dataflow and report components as shown in Figure 5-3.

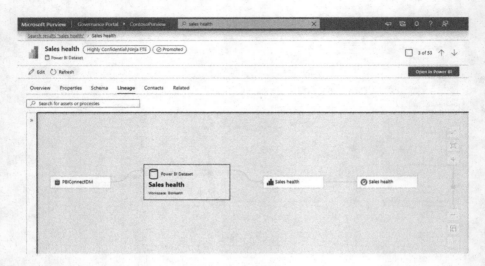

Figure 5-3. *Power BI lineage in Purview*

Additionally, the transformation and column level lineage of Power BI data are captured when running in Azure SQL Database as the source as shown in Figure 5-4. To see the details of the transformations, one can click on the Properties option and select the expression column.

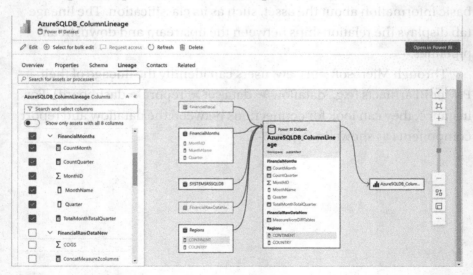

Figure 5-4. *Power BI lineage in Azure Database*

Introduction to Data Mapping in Microsoft Purview

A crucial part of data governance is data mapping, which involves identifying the connections and relationships between various sources and systems. Data management also relies on this process to understand how information is structured and utilized across different systems. Through its data mapping capabilities, Microsoft Purview platform provides organizations with a comprehensive view of their data. It enables them to manage their data assets while ensuring their integrity.

The Purview platform has numerous features, such as data sourcing discovery, data integration, metadata management, and data cataloging. These capabilities allow organizations to create a detailed view of their data, which can help them improve their data management and governance. This overview will talk about the different aspects of data mapping and how it can be used in Microsoft's platform.

Understanding Data Mapping

A data mapping process is a process that involves identifying the relationships between various data sources and their respective formats. It is essential to ensure that the data is accurately integrated and utilized across various systems. Microsoft Purview provides a framework for understanding how data flows between different systems. This process helps organizations identify how they can leverage the data they have.

Data mapping is a central component of Purview. It involves several activities.

- The process of data source discovery involves identifying all the sources of information within an organization, such as databases, data lakes, and cloud storage.

- Metadata management is a process that involves identifying and managing the associated metadata of data sources. This process helps organizations understand the structure and meanings of their data.

- A central repository of information assets that includes details about sources, types, and relationships is known as a data catalog. It serves as a reference for comprehending the data landscape and gaining access to it.

- The integration of data from various sources is defined as mapping the integration and transformation of that information. This entails establishing the relationships between elements and comprehending how information moves between the different systems.

Features of Data Mapping in Microsoft Purview

Microsoft Purview offers a variety of features for data mapping that are designed to help improve the management and governance of information.

- The central repository of Purview's data catalog allows users to organize and visualize their collected information assets. It includes details such as data classifications, lineages, and metadata.

- With the help of Purview's automatic extraction feature, users can easily get rid of the tedious process of gathering metadata from their sources. This ensures that their information assets are updated and reflect the current state of their relationships and structures.

- Through its data classification feature, Purview can help users identify and categorize their collected information assets according to their relevance and sensitivity. This helps in the development of effective data governance strategies.

- The Purview data lineage visualization offers a variety of visual representations of the information lineage, which helps users understand how their data is transported across various systems and transformations. This feature also helps users understand how their sources are utilized and processed.

- Users can customize the metadata attributes of their collected information assets to meet their specific business requirements. This allows them to obtain more accurate and timely information about their data.

- Through its integration with various data sources, such as on-premises databases and cloud platforms, Purview can provide users with visibility and comprehensive data mapping across diverse environments.

- With the ability to enforce and define various data governance policies, such as access controls and retention standards, Purview can help organizations manage their data mapping efforts.

View Data Map

Access `https://purview.microsoft.com/`. Choose data map feature of Microsoft Purview, and click Azure Portal as shown Figure 5-5.

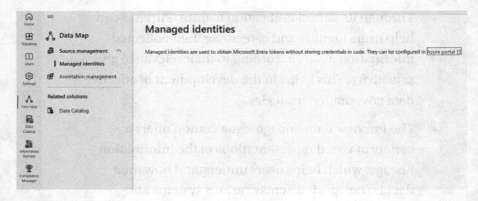

Figure 5-5. *Data map in Purview*

After you click the Azure Portal link in Figure 5-5, choose the type of source that you want to use. For instance, you can use Azure Cosmos DB Figure 5-6 and register source.

Figure 5-6. *Creation of source*

Navigate to the Microsoft Purview data map, and under source management, select source you want to view as shown in Figure 5-7.

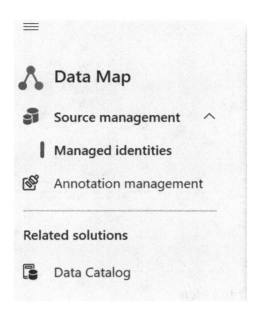

Figure 5-7. *Data source for data map*

Then, set the map view's default to "top," and click OK as shown in Figure 5-8. The map view allows you to view all of your collections and sources. It also lets you filter by collections, domains, and sources.

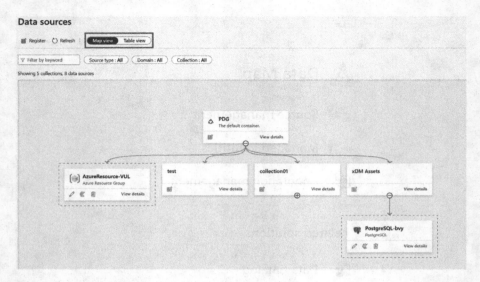

Figure 5-8. *Data map view*

From Figures 5-6, 5-7, and 5-8, we can view data map for any data source created in Microsoft Azure.

Benefits of Data Mapping in Microsoft Purview

Microsoft Purview data mapping solution provides organizations with numerous advantages.

- Through its data mapping capabilities, Purview helps organizations gain a deeper understanding of their data by providing a central view of its various relationships. This enables them to make more informed decisions and improve their efficiency.

- A data mapping process helps organizations integrate information from various sources. It involves identifying transformations and relationships and ensuring that data is utilized properly.

- Data mapping helps organizations maintain the quality of their information by ensuring that the correct integration and transformations are carried out. This eliminates the risk of errors and data inconsistencies.

- The enhanced capabilities of Purview data mapping allow organizations to develop and enforce data governance policies. These include providing insight into the relationships, structures, and classifications of their data.

- Companies can comply with regulations through data mapping, which provides them with a clear understanding of how their information flows and changes. This transparency can also help with compliance reporting.

- Purview's data management solution helps organizations reduce the manual work involved in managing their data by automating the extraction of metadata and creating a central catalog.

Practical Applications of Data Mapping in Microsoft Purview

Microsoft Purview can be used to map data in various scenarios. It can be used in various ways.

- Data integration and transformation: Data mapping is a process that enables organizations to create a unified view of their various data sources. For instance, a retailer might have multiple databases that contain customer information, sales data, and inventory data. With Purview, you can map these sources and define how they should be integrated. Through the integration of Purview and other data sources, a company can create reports and analyses that can provide insight into its customer behavior and sales performance.

- Data migration: Getting the most out of the migration process to modern platforms requires data mapping. This process can help organizations identify the relationships between their existing systems and the new cloud environment. In the case of a financial institution, data mapping can help determine the necessary changes to their data to ensure it is accurate and compliant.

- Data quality management: Through data mapping, an organization can gain a deeper understanding of how data is integrated and transformed. For instance, it can map patient data from different sources, such as lab results and electronic health records. This process can also help identify areas of concern that could affect the quality of data. Ensuring that the information used for reporting and patient care is reliable and accurate can help prevent costly errors.

- Compliance and auditing: Mapping data can help an organization comply with regulations such as the General Data Protection Regulation (GDPR). For instance, it can help an organization determine how its data is collected and stored. With Purview, it can also provide a clear audit trail that shows how the organization is following the regulations. This transparency can help the company avoid potential issues.

- Data governance and stewardship: Data mapping is also used to help organizations implement effective stewardship and governance policies. For instance, a public records agency can use Purview to map its data sources and create regulations that govern the quality and access of data. This process can help ensure that the organization is following proper procedures and that the information is being used properly.

Implementing Data Mapping in Microsoft Purview

Organizations should adopt best practices when it comes to mapping data in Microsoft Purview.

- Before implementing data mapping, it's important that the organization's goals are clear. This can help guide the process and ensure that the project is aligned with the company's needs. Having a clear understanding of the goals helps ensure that the project is carried out according to the plan.

- Using Purview's automated tools for data cataloging and extraction can help reduce the manual work involved in the mapping process. These tools can also ensure that the metadata is updated and accurate.

- Getting the input of various stakeholder groups, such as data owners, business users, and stewards, is also important in the mapping process. Their contributions can help with the identification of relationships and the alignment of the project with the business requirements.

- Data mapping documentation must be updated regularly to keep up with the changes in the structures and sources of information that affect the project. To ensure that the documentation is up to date, implement processes that allow for continuous review.

- Adopt policies that establish and enforce data governance, which includes the requirements for data quality, accessibility controls, and compliance. These help ensure that the practices of data mapping conform to the company's guidelines and are aimed at effectively managing information.

- Using Purview's visualization tools can help visualize and analyze the various relationships and data flows within a company's data. This can help improve the efficiency of the mapping process and enable better analysis and management.

Challenges and Considerations

Despite the advantages of data mapping within Microsoft Purview, it is important that organizations take the necessary steps to address the challenges that come with it.

- Mapping intricate data structures in complicated data sets can be challenging, especially when there are numerous sources and transformations. To effectively handle such scenarios, organizations may require the addition of resources or tools.

- In addition to having the necessary tools and resources, organizations also need to ensure that their data mapping practices are in compliance with security and privacy laws. This can be done through the implementation of appropriate access controls and measures.

- Misinformation or inaccuracies in data can affect the development and implementation of data mapping projects. To ensure that the mapping process is carried out according to the correct data, organizations should regularly address these issues.

- In addition to having the necessary tools and resources, organizations also need to ensure that their data mapping practices are in compliance with security and privacy laws. This can be done through the implementation of appropriate access controls and measures.

Microsoft Purview's data mapping feature is designed to help organizations improve their efficiency and effectiveness when it comes to managing their data. It provides a detailed view of their data structures and relationships. The platform's features, such as data cataloging and automated extraction, allow organizations to create updated and accurate mappings, which can help them comply with regulations and improve their quality management.

Data mapping can be carried out in Purview by defining goals, utilizing tools, and working with stakeholders. Although it can be challenging to create and maintain accurate mappings due to privacy and complex environments, the advantages of doing so are numerous. Organizations can attain improved data visibility, make their governance practices more effective, and improve their business outcomes by utilizing the platform's capabilities. Data mapping is an integral part of data management techniques, and in Microsoft Purview, it serves as the foundation for comprehending transformations, integrations, and flows. It also supports data governance and ensures transparency and integrity.

CHAPTER 6

Data Insights and Analytics

In the previous chapter, we have covered topics such as data lineage and data mapping features of data governance solution of Microsoft Purview. We will be covering introductions, understandings, features, benefits, practical applications, implementation, challenges, and considerations of data lineage and data mapping, respectively. In this chapter, we will take deep dive into reporting and analytics module of Microsoft Purview. We will be covering Microsoft's Data Health Management suite such as control, data quality, actions, and reports. Further, health management reports in Microsoft Purview such as sensitivity label insights about your data in Microsoft Purview, data stewardship, and catalog adoption dashboard in Microsoft Purview.

Introduction

The process of health management involves continuously improving and maintaining an organization's data quality and accessibility. This discipline is vital to ensuring that information is obtainable, secure, and accurate. It's similar to how healthcare organizations strive to maintain the overall health of their patients.

© Charles Waghmare 2025
C. Waghmare, *Introducing Microsoft Purview*,
https://doi.org/10.1007/979-8-8688-1204-0_6

Health management is an important discipline within an organization. It involves continuously improving and enhancing the accessibility and quality of information within an organization. Data that is reliable and high quality can help businesses make informed decisions. High-quality data can also help organizations reduce the time and resources that they spend on correcting errors. Health management's risk management discipline can also help minimize the effects of data breaches and regulatory noncompliance. Having good data can also give organizations a competitive edge, allowing them to take advantage of artificial intelligence, machine learning, and analytics. Trust is also built when data is protected and accurate. The goal of health management is to ensure that the security, integrity, and reliability of an organization's information are maintained at all times.

Microsoft's Data Health Management suite provides various tools and components that can help you develop and implement effective data governance strategies. These are control, data quality, actions, and reports as shown in Figure 6-1.

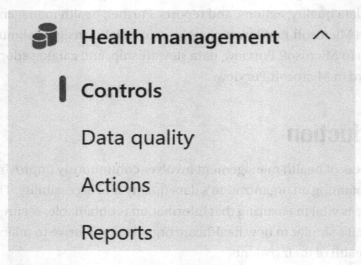

Figure 6-1. *Microsoft's Data Health Management*

Various components shown in Figure 6-1 are part of Microsoft Purview's information governance platform by navigating to the "Data Catalog" and selecting the "Health Management" drop-down. This section will provide a brief overview of each of the tools, their scope, and how they can be used to improve your knowledge of your data.

Control

Through controls, data officers and data stewards can assess the health of their information assets. They can set global standards and implement procedures that meet specific requirements of their organization. This approach can be used to address the needs of various groups within an organization. In order to improve the effectiveness of your data estate, you can customize the settings and health thresholds. You can also set the frequency of data updates that are performed on your active controls. Figure 6-2 shows an example of health control dashboard.

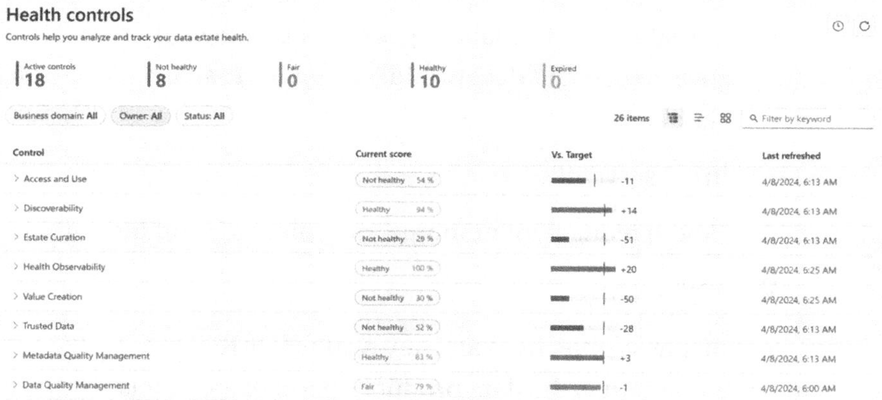

Figure 6-2. *Health control dashboard*

From Figure 6-2, below are some health controls in Microsoft Purview:

- Access and use
  - Self-serve access enablement is the percentage of products that have enabled self-service workflows and policies.
  - Compliant data use is the percentage of all data subscriptions that have a stated data use purpose.

- Discoverability
  - Data cataloging is a data product owner's percentage of their products being published in the governance domain.
  - Data products connection is the percentage of data products with mapped data assets.

- Estate curation
  - Classification and labeling is the percentage of governance and data product domains that are classified.

- Health observability
  - Health management monitoring, alerting, and insights.

- Value creation
  - Business objectives and key results (OKR) alignment is the data product's percentage that is aligned with an organization's OKRs.

- Trusted data

  - Data product ownership is the percentage of data products that have owners assigned.

  - Data quality enablement is data product's quality score that is calculated by considering the various factors that affect its operation.

  - Data product certification is percentage of data products that are certified by an authorized owner within the governance domain.

- Metadata quality management

  - Data product useability is data products that have at least a hundred characters' worth of descriptions that are included in this category. These include a parent domain with over a hundred characters' worth of descriptions and a glossary term that has at least 25 characters.

  - Linked assets is the data product's percentage that includes a linked asset and a published glossary term is considered to be noteworthy.

Through controls, data officers and data stewards can assess the health of their information assets. They can set global standards and implement procedures that meet specific requirements of their organization. This approach can be used to address the needs of various groups within an organization. In order to improve the effectiveness of your data estate, you can customize the settings and health thresholds. You can also set the frequency of data updates that are performed on your active controls. As shown in Figure 6-3, from a control group or hovering over it, select the Edit "Pencil" button to change the control's settings.

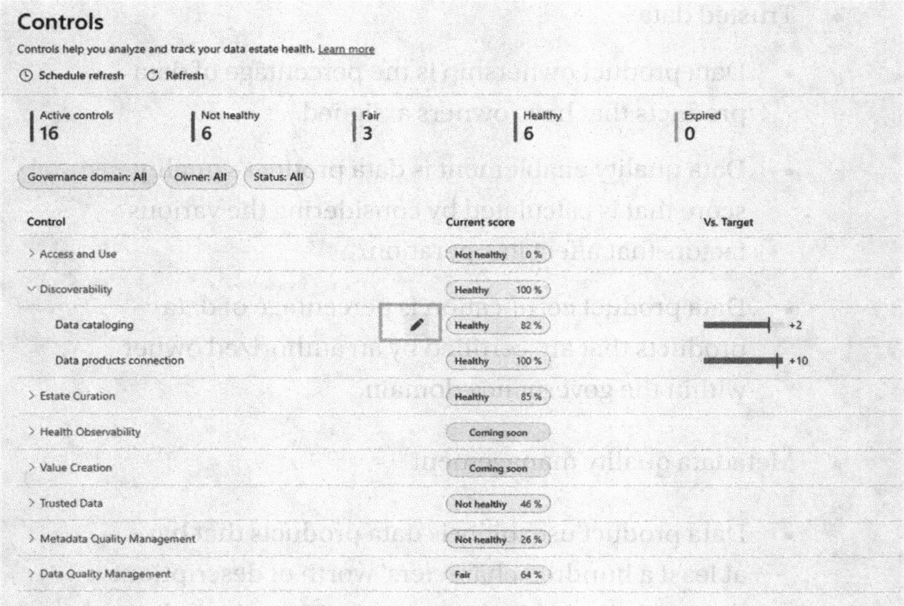

Figure 6-3. *Edit health control dashboard*

Then as shown in Figure 6-3, add owner name, control description, and domain names. Select the Save button to save your changes.

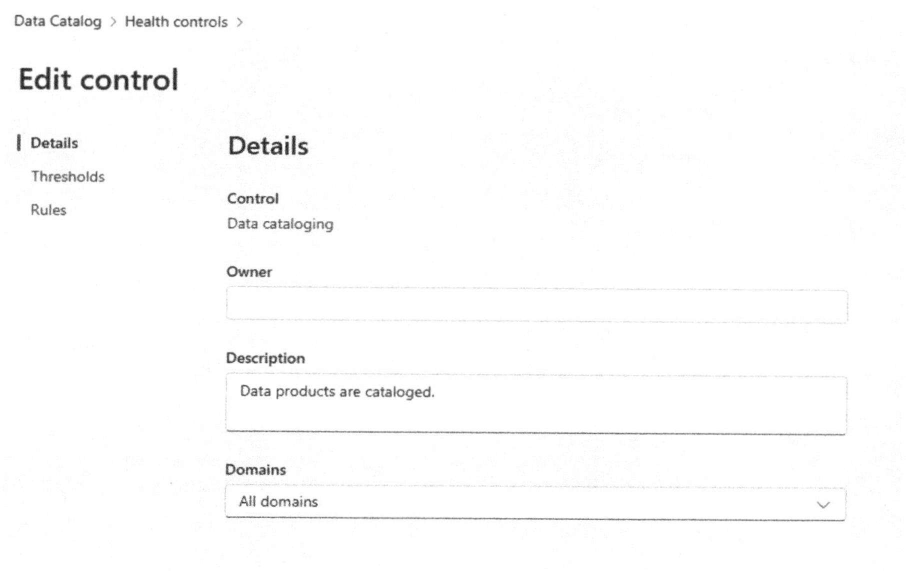

Data Catalog > Health controls >

Edit control

| Details

Thresholds

Rules

Details

Control
Data cataloging

Owner

Description

Data products are cataloged.

Domains

All domains   ⌄

Figure 6-4. *Update health control dashboard*

From a group or hovering over it, choose the control and click the Edit button to edit Thresholds tab as shown in Figure 6-5.

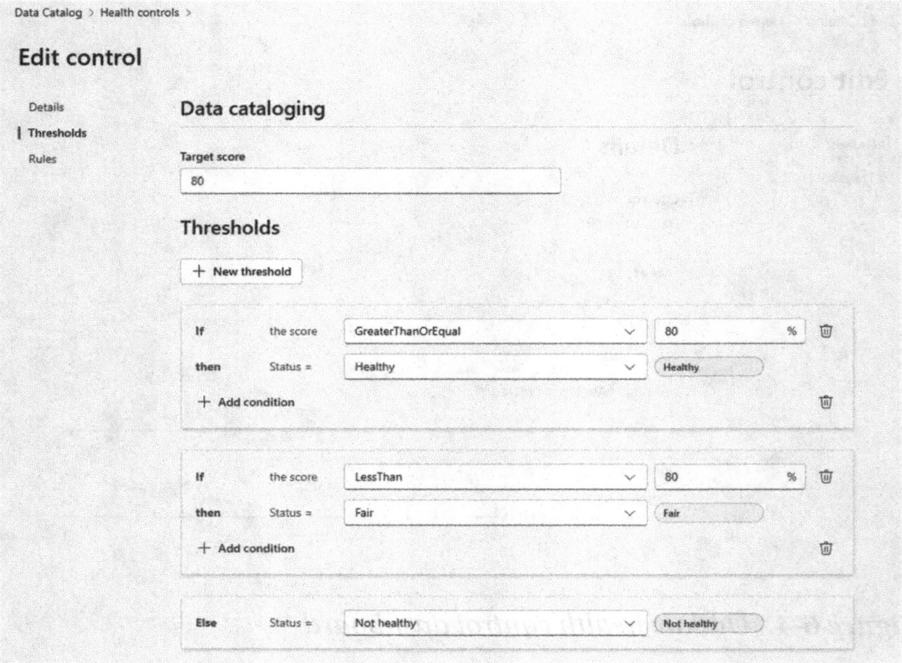

Figure 6-5. *Update thresholds in health control dashboard*

Data Quality

The Microsoft Purview data quality solution helps data owners and governance teams identify and improve the integrity of their data. This is very important as it allows them to make informed decisions and improve the efficiency of their operations. Without reliable data, organizations can't effectively utilize AI systems.

The lack of reliable data can affect the efficiency of organizations' decision-making and business processes. With the help of Microsoft Purview data quality, users can easily evaluate and improve the quality of their data by implementing rules that are not only low-code but also AI-generated. These rules are then applied to the various data domains to provide a comprehensive view of the data quality.

The Purview data quality solution includes AI-powered capabilities, which can recommend columns for profiling. This feature allows humans to intervene and improve the recommendations. In addition to enhancing the profiling's accuracy, this iterative process also helps the underlying models get better. Figure 6-6 is an illustration of data quality dashboard

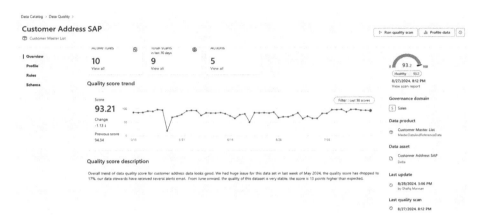

Figure 6-6. *Data quality dashboard*

Organizations can enhance, measure, and improve the data quality through the use of Microsoft Purview data quality. This solution helps organizations foster confidence in using AI in their decision-making processes and improve the reliability of their insights.

Actions

Through health actions, data governance professionals can access critical insights that can be easily tracked and analyzed. These actions can be triggered by health controls and can help them identify and address issues that are affecting their organizations as shown in Figure 6-7.

Health actions

Optimize your data health with these actions. Learn more

Active   In progress   Resolved   My items

Total action items	High severity	Medium severity	Low severity
167	56	84	27

Assigned to: All   Business domain: All   Active since: All   Finding type: All   Finding subtype: All   Severity: All   Add filter

7 items   Filter by keyword

Finding type ↑	Total findings	Severity breakdown	Finding subtype
Access and Use	18		Compliant data use
Data Quality	13		Data asset quality rule score, +3 more
Data Quality Management	40		Data asset quality rule score, +3 more
Discoverability	7		Data cataloging
Estate Curation	16		Classification and labeling
Metadata Quality Management	20		Data product usability, +1 more
Trusted Data	53		Data product certification, +2 more

Figure 6-7. *Action dashboard*

Data stewards can filter the actions they view by category, type, and name. They can also assign tasks to specific individuals and see the results. These actions are brought up to date as they are derived from the health controls. **Note:** Data stewards can create, update, and read policies and artifacts in their governance domain. You can also examine policies and artifacts from other domains.

Reports

As shown in Figure 6-8, the data governance office stewards and analysts can easily access out-of-the-box reports to gain deeper insight into their organization's data. These reports provide summaries of various business concepts, such as data products and governance domains, but also focus on your data governance goals and catalog adoption.

Reports

Total reports	Active reports	Draft reports
8	8	0

8 items   Filter by keyword

Report name	Report type	Last updated	Status
Assets	System	4/8/2024, 6:28 AM	● Active
Catalog adoption	System	4/8/2024, 6:28 AM	● Active
Classifications	System	4/8/2024, 6:28 AM	● Active
Data governance	System	4/8/2024, 6:28 AM	● Active
Data stewardship	System	4/8/2024, 6:28 AM	● Active
Glossary	System	4/8/2024, 6:28 AM	● Active
Sensitivity labels	System	4/8/2024, 6:28 AM	● Active

Figure 6-8. *Out-of-the-box reports*

These reports allow organizations to effectively manage, protect, and govern their data in a way that aligns with their business and regulatory needs. Additionally, users can create custom reports to suit specific requirements using integrations with tools like Microsoft Power BI.

In Microsoft Purview, access to certain governance domains is granted to business users and data experts who have specific permissions. These roles allow them to manage and read the objects in these domains. The following are the roles that are currently available in Microsoft Purview data catalog.

- Governance domain owner: Ability to delegate all the other governance permissions for your domain. You can also configure data quality scans and access policies.

- Governance domain reader: Ability to monitor and analyze the operations of your governance domains.

- Data steward: Ability to create, update, or read policies and artifacts in their respective domains. You can additionally examine the policies and artifacts from other domains.

- Data product owner: Ability to create, update, and read the data products in their governance domain. They can also examine the artifacts from other domains.

- Data catalog reader: Look through the published concepts in the catalog for all your governance domains.

- Data quality stewards: Able to choose various features of the data quality suite, such as data profiling, rule management, and data quality scanning. They can also configure alert and threshold settings.

- Data quality reader: Browse through the various data quality insight features, such as the definition of data quality rules and the data quality error files. However, this role cannot perform data profiling.

- Data quality metadata reader: This role cannot perform data profiling. It only browses through the various features of the data quality suite, such as the definition of data quality rules and the data quality error files.

- Data profile steward: This role can run data profiling jobs and can access the details of profiling insight. It can also monitor jobs and browse through all of the data quality insights. However, this does not allow you to perform data quality scanning or create rules.

- Data profile reader: It requires permissions to browse through the various features of data quality insight and drill down to the details of its results.

- Data health owner: Create, update, and read health management artifacts.

- Data health reader: Can read artifacts in health management.

Health Management Reports in Microsoft Purview

With health management reports, your users can easily explore and analyze your health data. They can also create custom reports for your business.

Sensitivity Label Insights About Your Data in Microsoft Purview

Similar to subject tags, classification labels identify a specific type of information within an organization's data estate. They can also be used to describe the sensitive nature of certain data. For instance, if a project's name is highly confidential within an organization, then sensitivity labels might be used to describe the information that other organizations are privy to.

A classification label is matched directly to a specific type of information, such as a Social Security number. On the other hand, a sensitivity label is applied when conditions and classifications are found together. This type of label refers to the various parameters that can be used to describe the data that you have stored.

Similar to what's used in Microsoft 365 services and apps, the data estate of Microsoft Purview uses classification labels. This allows you to extend the scope of your sensitivity labels to include other assets in the data mapping. To access sensitivity label report, go to the Health Management drop-down and select Reports. Then, select the Sensitivity labels to view the report as shown in Figure 6-9.

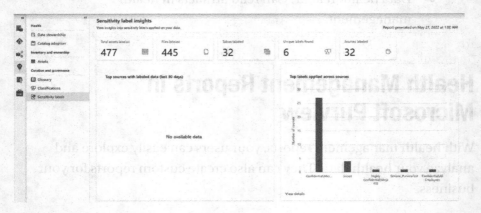

Figure 6-9. *Sensity label reports*

Get Insights into Data Stewardship from Microsoft Purview

The data stewardship report is part of the Data Estate Insights app's health section and provides a convenient way for users to get in touch with their data governance and quality concerns. It also offers a variety of tools and resources to help them make informed decisions. Through the Data Estate Insights, users can get an overview of the various assets in the data map and identify gaps that can be closed to improve the data estate's governance.

To navigate to the Purview portal, go to the Microsoft site and click on the "General" button. As shown show in Figure 6-10, select the Health Management drop-down, and then select Reports, and then, select Data Stewardship. This dashboard is designed for data scientists and other quality-focused users who require a deeper understanding of how their organizations are managing their health. It also shows high-level KPIs that can help them reduce risk.

As shown in Figure 6-10, the three categories of asset curation are "fully curated," "partly curated," and "not curated." They are based on the various attributes that are present in an asset. For instance, if an asset has multiple classification tags and an assigned Data Owner, then it is considered fully curated. On the other hand, if all of these are not present, then it is not curated. Data ownership refers to the ownership of an asset. The blank assets in the Contacts tab are labeled as "No owner" while the ones that have an assigned Data Owner are referred to as "Owner assigned."

Figure 6-10. *Asset curation and asset ownership in data stewardship dashboard*

As shown in Figure 6-11, a health management scorecard is a set of tools that help organizations improve their governance by understanding key performance indicators. It can be used by data scientists and other management professionals to make informed decisions.

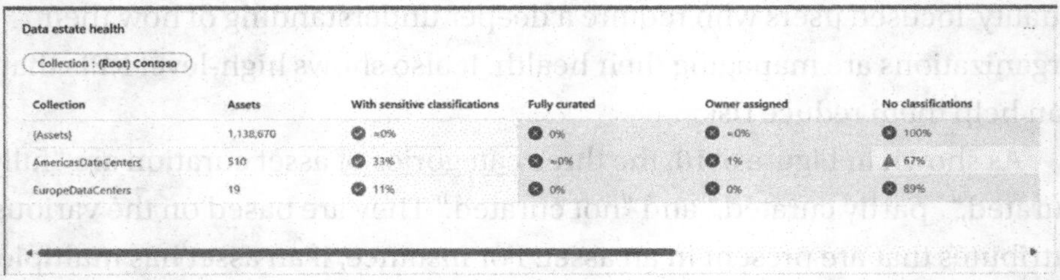

| Data estate health | | | | | |
| Collection : (Root) Contoso | | | | | |
Collection	Assets	With sensitive classifications	Fully curated	Owner assigned	No classifications
(Assets)	1,138,670	≈0%	0%	≈0%	100%
AmericasDataCenters	510	33%	≈0%	1%	67%
EuropeDataCenters	19	11%	0%	0%	89%

Figure 6-11. *Health management scorecard in data stewardship dashboard*

The count of assets is collection by drilling down. The sensitive classification of assets indicates their count with regard to any system's classification. The count of fully curated assets is computed by considering the various characteristics of an asset, such as its data owner and classification. The owner assigned category refers to the count of assets with the data owner on them. No classifications imply that there are no designated categories for the assets.

Asset curation exists in three buckets of data assets: fully curated, partially curated, and not curated as shown in Figure 6-12. These are based on the attributes that have been given to them. A fully curated asset is one that has at least one attribute that's related to it, such as a classification tag or a description. When none of the linked attributes are present, the piece is considered partially curated, while when all of them are absent, it is labeled as not curated.

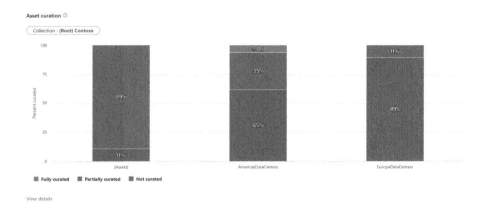

Figure 6-12. *Asset curation in data stewardship dashboard*

Catalog Adoption from Microsoft Purview

As shown in Figure 6-13, the adoption dashboard features various charts for easy identification as follows:

- The number of people using your data catalog in the last month is also displayed in the dashboard.

- The total number of searches performed in the last month is shown in the dashboard.

- The dashboard also displays the various features that are being used by the users of your data catalog.

- Most viewed assets.

- The most searched terms in your data catalog are displayed in the dashboard.

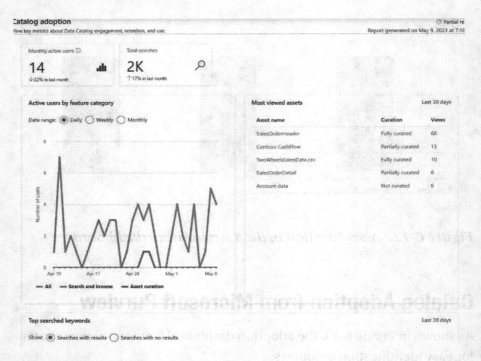

Figure 6-13. *Adoption dashboard*

Monthly Active Users

In Figure 6-13, the count of active users in Microsoft Purview data catalog is shown by the monthly active users' chart. It shows the number of people who have performed various actions in the last 30 days. These include searching for a term, updating an asset, and browsing the catalog. The chart also displays a percentage change in the number of users from the previous month, as well as an indication of a growing or decreasing trend.

Total Searches

In Figure 6-13, the total searches tile shows the number of searches made in the last 30 days in Microsoft Purview data catalog. The lower part displays an indication of a decrease or increase in the activity from the previous month.

Active Users by Feature Category

In Figure 6-13, category chart for active users can help you monitor the activity of your users in the data catalog. The chart's top section allows you to view the activity of your users on a weekly, daily, or monthly basis.

Most Viewed Assets

In Figure 6-13, the table shows the most viewed assets in your database. It represents the sum of views over the past 30 days. Although the table provides the most viewed assets' information, it also displays other details. The three possible statuses of an asset's classification are "fully curated," "partially curated," and "not curated." The first is based on the data owner and the number of classification tags that it has. If none of these are present, then the asset is considered not curated. The data stewardship dashboard provides a more detailed view of the asset's condition. The count of views that an asset has received in the last 30 days is known as views.

Top Searched Keywords

In Figure 6-14, the table shows the top search terms that were used in a particular query, as well as those that didn't produce results. This helps you understand the users' searches and what they're looking for.

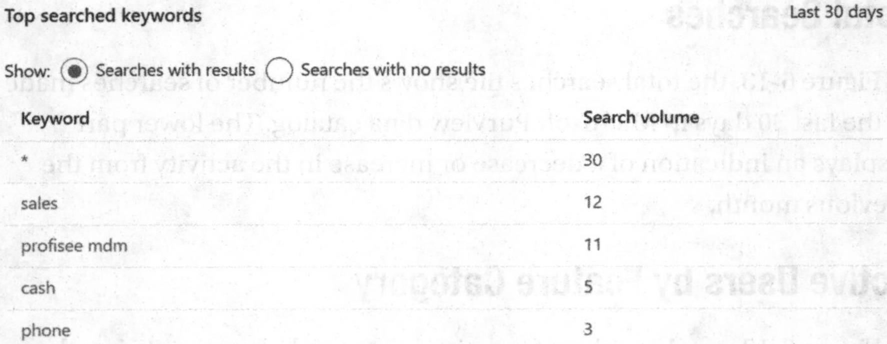

Top searched keywords   Last 30 days

Show: (●) Searches with results   ( ) Searches with no results

Keyword	Search volume
*	30
sales	12
profisee mdm	11
cash	5
phone	3

Figure 6-14. Top searched keywords

The table's top row displays the radio buttons that allow you to choose between displaying keywords that have produced results or those that did not. In the data catalog, you can pick the appropriate keywords to conduct the search, and you can examine the results for yourself. The volume of searches for the given keyword is displayed in the table. It represents the number of times the term was searched within the last 30 days.

With this, we have come to the end of this chapter. We have presented a variety of reports and activities related to the health management suite of Microsoft, including data quality, control, and reports. In addition, we have also discussed the adoption dashboard and sensitivity label insights in Microsoft Purview. In the next chapter, we will explore policy management and compliance solution to provide a framework for regulatory requirements. This will cover defining information governance policies and policy enforcement mechanisms and ensuring compliance with regulatory requirements such as GDPR and CCPA.

CHAPTER 7

Compliance in Microsoft Purview

In the previous chapter, we have presented various reports and activities about Microsoft's health management suite, including data quality and control. In addition, we talked about the sensitivity label insights and adoption dashboard in Microsoft Purview. Next, we will look into Microsoft Purview compliance solution that can help organizations meet their regulatory requirements. This will cover the various aspects of compliance, such as Communication Compliance, data lifecycle management compliance or managing information protection, records management, and eDiscovery. Finally, we will use these concepts to ensure that organizations are following the requirements of the CCPA and GDPR. In short, we will be exploring core component of Microsoft Purview called as information compliance as shown in Figure 7-1.

© Charles Waghmare 2025
C. Waghmare, *Introducing Microsoft Purview*,
https://doi.org/10.1007/979-8-8688-1204-0_7

Figure 7-1. *Core components of Microsoft Purview*

Introduction

The Purview suite of compliance management solutions from Microsoft helps organizations manage their information and comply with regulations. This section provides a quick overview of the offerings and how they can help you meet your organization's compliance goals. One of the most common concerns of compliance and security professionals is Insider risks. According to studies, these risks are typically associated with specific activities or events. It can be hard to identify and prevent these types of risks due to the variety of vulnerabilities they can expose your organization to.

Figure 7-2 shows the offerings of Microsoft Purview suite of compliance and risk management solutions; organizations can easily manage their data risk and comply with these offerings.

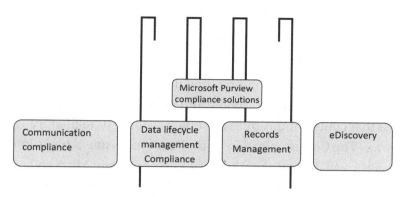

Figure 7-2. *Microsoft Purview compliance solution*

In the upcoming section, we will be exploring each of these solutions such as Communication Compliance, data lifecycle management compliance or managing information protection, records management, and eDiscovery, in depth.

Communication Compliance

Microsoft Purview Communication Compliance is a tool that helps organizations identify and prevent violations of various regulations, such as the GDPR and CCPA. It can also help them manage their risk of unauthorized access and distribution of confidential or sensitive information. User pseudonyms are used in the system, and investigators are assigned a role based on their access controls.

One of the most important factors that businesses consider when it comes to complying with internal regulations is the protection of their sensitive information. With the help of Microsoft Purview Communication Compliance, they can quickly detect and prevent harassment incidents. It can also take action to minimize the risks associated with certain types of communication, such as email and Microsoft Teams. These types of communication can include inappropriate and threatening messages, as well as communications that share confidential data outside the organization.

The Microsoft Purview solution provides an insider risk assessment that enables organizations to identify and respond to problematic messages that could compromise their data security or regulatory compliance. The Communication Compliance assessment looks into the messages sent and received by third-party apps and Microsoft services, such as Teams and Microsoft 365 Copilot. It can then identify potential policy violations, including the sharing of confidential data or inappropriate language. It can also prevent violations of capital gains and stock manipulation rules.

The goal of Communication Compliance is to promote secure and compliant communication across all enterprise channels. Investigators can take corrective actions, such as removing problematic messages from Microsoft Teams or alerting senders to inappropriate conduct, with the help of role-based access controls. With the help of Communication Compliance, organizations can now detect and resolve potential regulatory and business violations. It can also help them manage the risks associated with certain types of communication.

Classifications for various types of harassment are provided by Microsoft Purview Communication Compliance. These include discrimination, threat, and targeted harassment. Some of the common types of regulatory compliance violations that can be identified include corporate sabotage, gift and entertainment requests, stock manipulation, and money laundering.

The Microsoft Purview Communication Compliance solution helps minimize the risk of unauthorized messages in your organization by detecting and acting on them. It can also help you monitor and analyze external and internal communications for compliance.

Through the Microsoft Purview solution, reviewers can easily identify and analyze the various types of communications that are used by your organization. They can then take appropriate actions to ensure that they're in compliance with the company's message standards. With the help of Microsoft 365 communication policies, you can easily address the following various challenges that come with managing and monitoring external and internal communications:

- The rising volume of message data has prompted organizations to rethink their approach to managing internal and external communications.

- To keep track of the increasing number of communication channels, organizations are now looking into the various types of channels that they use.

- The increasing number of channels and the potential fines they could face have prompted many organizations to rethink their strategies regarding the management of internal and external communication.

One of the most common changes that organizations make regarding their communication policies is the separation of the roles of the IT group and the compliance management team. This allows the latter to focus on the review and investigation of messages, while the former can set up policies and roles. For instance, the IT group might be responsible for the creation of policies and groups, while the compliance management team might be responsible for the review and mitigation of messages.

Communication Compliance Scenarios Designed to Help Organizations

A communication policy can be used to review messages in your company in various compliance categories as below such as risk management, corporate policies, and regulatory compliance.

Risk Management

As a company, you are responsible for all communications that are distributed across your network systems and infrastructure. Having a communication policy can help identify potential risks and minimize the damage they can do to your company's operations. For instance, you can check messages for unauthorized discussions about certain projects or conflicts of interest.

Corporate Policies

In order to maintain a positive and ethical work environment, every user must follow company policies and standards in all communications. Having a Communication Compliance policy can help identify potential issues and prevent them from happening in the first place. For instance, it can help prevent employees from using offensive language or harassing other people.

Regulatory Compliance

As part of their regular operations, many companies also follow certain regulatory standards. These standards often require them to establish procedures that are designed to monitor the quality of their communications. One of the most common examples of a requirement that an organization must follow is the FINRA Rule 3110, which requires them to have a process that is designed to check the effectiveness of their messaging. One of the most common requirements that an organization must meet is the requirement to review its communications with its broker-dealers in order to prevent potential violations of the securities laws. Having a Communication Compliance program can help them meet this requirement.

Several below key features are included in Communication Compliance to help organizations address their messaging platform compliance issues.

- Intelligent customizable templates

- Flexible remediation workflows

- Actionable insights

- Intelligent customizable templates

Intelligent customizable templates: With the help of intelligent communication templates, you can implement machine learning to automatically detect and prevent communication violations within your organization. Communication policies can be customized to address the most common risks. With predefined templates, they can be created and updated more quickly to address issues related to sensitive information, regulatory compliance, and inappropriate content.

New machine learning capabilities can help automate the detection and mitigation of various communication violations, such as discrimination, harassment, and profanity. They can also help reduce the time it takes to investigate and resolve these issues. The new condition builder feature can help simplify the creation and application of policies by allowing users to configure their conditions in a single interface.

Flexible remediation workflows: A new workflow for quick action on policy matches allows you to act immediately. It also lets you send notifications to users with matching policies.

Policy matches are grouped in conversations to help you identify which messages are related to your communication rules. For instance, in the Pending tab, all messages in a given channel will be displayed with matching policies. On the other hand, those that aren't related to your rules won't be shown. The keyword highlighting feature in the message text section helps reviewers quickly identify and analyze the conditions that match your policy. Text analysis using optical character recognition can be performed on handwritten and printed text in attached images or emails. New message filters help speed up the analysis and remediation of policy alerts. These can be used for different fields, such as sender, recipient, date, and domains. New message views make it easier to investigate and perform remediation actions. Attachments can also be viewed to provide context during the remediation process.

The historical view of all the user messages that have been sent or escalated for policy matches provides a more contextualized view of the process. It also allows reviewers to easily identify repeat or first-time policies. A pattern-based notification is also shown in the notifications section to help identify recurring behavior patterns. This type of notification helps raise awareness of the issues that are related to your policy.

Review messages in different languages with the help of translate support. All the details are automatically translated into the reviewer's language. The attachment detection feature can help you identify and analyze the linked content in Microsoft Teams and OneDrive that matches the conditions and policies of your organization. It can also extract the content for detailed review. Investigators can save time and effort by summarizing lengthy emails, chats, and Viva Engage or Teams messages with the help of Microsoft Copilot in Purview. It can create a comprehensive summary of the exchange, including transcripts, attachments, and recordings.

Actionable Insights

New interactive dashboards allow you to quickly view the status of your organization's various alerts and policies. New features for proactive notifications include automatic email updates for policy matches that require immediate attention. Also, dashboards for prioritized items are now available. The new interactive dashboards provide a variety of information about policies and users, such as their trends and pending actions. We can easily export a full log of your review and policy activities from Microsoft Purview to help support audit requests.

With the integration of Microsoft 365 services, organizations can now easily review and resolve compliance issues by monitoring and capturing messages across various communication channels.

Private and public Microsoft Teams channels can now benefit from the support of individual chats and group conversations in compliance with the standards of Microsoft 365. Also, you can detect group and individual conversations in meetings transcripts. To implement a policy for group and individual conversations, you must first add the groups, users, or distribution channels to the list. Users can also report inappropriate messages in group and private conversations. These messages can then be reviewed and remediated.

All Exchange Online mailboxes can now be analyzed for compliance issues. Instant access to attachments and emails matching the conditions of the communication policy can be obtained for investigation. As a source channel, Exchange Online is no longer required.

The Copilot and Microsoft 365 Copilot tools can now detect interactions that were initiated by users in Microsoft 365. These activities are then analyzed for compliance.

Public and private conversations within Viva Engage can now be monitored and analyzed for compliance. The channel is also optional and can only be used in native mode to check messages and attachments.

Mailboxes in Microsoft 365 can be imported with data from third-party sources, which can be checked for compliance. Connections to popular platforms, such as Instant Bloomberg, can also be monitored and analyzed.

Below recommended actions guide can help you get started with implementing and managing Communication Compliance. It provides a variety of steps such as configure, investigate, remediate, and monitor as shown in Figure 7-3 that can help you establish and manage policies and distribution groups.

Figure 7-3. *Steps to manage communication compliance*

Before you start implementing and updating policies in configure steps, you must identify and configure your Communication Compliance requirements. Having a template for policies can help you quickly modify and update them as needed. For example, testing a policy for the distribution of potentially offensive content in group discussions is ideal before implementing it for everyone.

The next step of investigation is to identify and configure policies that will comply with your organization's communication requirements. This step involves performing various tasks such as reviewing the user activity history and issuing alerts.

The remediation process involves addressing communication issues that you identified using methods such as the "Remediate option. These include alerting the user, segregating messages, removing them from the teams, and investigating them.

The entire process monitoring of Communication Compliance monitoring involves keeping track of and mitigating the issues that were identified by the policies. As the investigations and remediation actions are carried out, the existing policies may need to be updated or modified.

Data Lifecycle Management Compliance

The Microsoft Purview data management platform provides you with the tools and capabilities to manage your data lifecycle. It allows you to retain and remove the content that's required for regulatory compliance and business purposes, while also reducing risk and liability.

One of the most critical factors that businesses need to consider when it comes to data lifecycle management is the availability of their content. This is done through the use of retention policies, which can be used for various Microsoft 365 workloads such as Exchange, SharePoint, and OneDrive. One of the most flexible options that businesses can use is to configure their policy to automatically remove the content after a certain period. This can be done by combining the two actions into one. For instance, if you want to retain email for a period of three years, then you can choose to remove it after that.

A retention policy can be customized to target various instances within an organization, such as all of your company's mailboxes and all of your SharePoint sites. It can also be used to only retain specific instances, such as those for specific regions or departments. If you have specific requirements for the retention of specific types of content, such as legal documents, you can create and implement retention labels that can be applied to apps. Users can then inspect the content to determine its retention period.

One of the most important features of a mailbox archiving solution is the ability to store additional space for users. It can also be used to automatically expand the storage capacity of your mailbox for those that need more than 100 GB. A default email archiving policy will automatically move all of your emails to an archive mailbox. It can be customized to meet specific requirements. Mailboxes that are inactive after staff members leave can still retain their content. You can also import PST files using network upload or the drive shipping method.

Microsoft Purview Records Management

Microsoft Purview records management is a tool that helps organizations manage their legal obligations and comply with regulations. It can also help them reduce their costs and improve their efficiency by regularly disposing of nonessential items. Microsoft Purview records management capabilities are file plan, retention labels for individual items, retention policies if needed for baseline retention, and disposition review and proof of disposition.

With **file plan**, you can create and import retention labels either interactively or in bulk. You can also export for analysis. Optional administrative data can be added to labels to help with the identification and tracking of regulatory or business requirements. **Retention labels** can be used to set up a flexible schedule for the retention and deletion of records. It can be used automatically or manually. **Disposition review and proof of disposition** allows manual review of content before getting deleted permanently with proof of records disposition.

Compliance Solution for eDiscovery

eDiscovery is a process utilized in legal proceedings to identify and retrieve electronic data. It can be used to help prove or disprove a case. Microsoft Purview eDiscovery is a preview that lets you manage and identify the content in Microsoft 365 services. It supports various services in Microsoft 365, such as Exchange Online, Teams, OneDrive, and SharePoint. Through the eDiscovery search feature, you can look for sites and mailboxes in the same search. Also, you can examine and export the content in sites and mailboxes.

Capabilities of eDiscovery

In this subsection, we are planning to cover capabilities and features of eDiscovery in details so that reader will have thorough knowledge to apply them in their day-to-day work.

Search for content: With search for content feature, you can find all of the content that's in your OneDrive accounts, Exchange mailboxes, Microsoft Teams, and various other groups and platforms through this feature.

Keyword queries and search conditions: Use a keyword query language to create customized searches for content terms that meet specific criteria. You can also set conditions to narrow down your search results.

Search statistics and samples: Upon completing a search query, you can view the estimated results, including the total number of items that came up as well as the size of each one. A sampling of the products featured in the search results can also be viewed.

Export search results: You can export your search results to local computers of your organization. When exporting results, the items are packaged and copied from their original location. They will then be downloaded to a local computer as the export package.

Case management. All the information related to a particular investigation is stored in an eDiscovery case. Members can be assigned to a case to manage who can see and access its contents.

Role-based access permissions (RBAC): With RBAC permissions, you can set the tasks that your users can perform on eDiscovery. You can create custom eDiscovery role groups or a built-in group that handles specific permissions.

Advanced indexing: When a search, export, or review process is conducted, the associated content points are reindexed using advanced indexing. With advanced indexing, any content that was deemed partially indexed is automatically reprocessed to make it easier to find when investigating.

Review set: A review set is created and managed by Microsoft using the Azure storage cloud. It is secure and can store relevant data. Whenever you add data to an evaluation set, it is replicated to the review repository from the collected items' original location. A review set is a static, well-defined collection of content that can be searched, filtered, tagged, and predicted to provide relevant results. Reports can be generated regarding the changes made to the review set.

Support for cloud attachments and SharePoint versions: When creating a review set, you may add linked or cloud files as part of the content. You can also add all the versions of a particular document to the review set. The target file of an attached cloud file or linked file is automatically added to the review group. You can also include the latest versions of a specific document in the set.

Optical character recognition (OCR): When a review set is updated with new content, OCR automatically extracts the text from the images and includes it in the review set. This feature allows users to search for text based on the image in the review set.

Conversation threading: When a chat message from Viva Engage or Teams is added to a review group, it will automatically collect the rest of the conversation thread. The entire chat will be added to the review group once it has items that meet the search criteria. This feature allows users to review the items in the back and forth discussions.

Search statistics and reports: You can view the statistics related to the items that were retrieved using the search query or add them to a review set. These include the number of items that were returned, the content locations of the most searched items, and the search criteria that led to the results. A subset of the results can also be previewed.

Review set filtering: Once content has been added to a review set, filters will be applied to only display the items that comply with your specific criteria. You can then save the filters as a query so that they can be easily applied later. With the saved queries and review set filters, you can quickly find the most relevant content for your specific investigation.

Tagging: By using tags, you can identify the most relevant and nonrelevant content. When attorneys, experts, and other users examine a particular piece of content, their thoughts on it are captured using tags.

For instance, users can tag documents with the word "nonresponsive" if the goal is to exclude irrelevant content. After the content has been tagged and reviewed, a review query can be generated to exclude the nonresponsive content. This process can help eliminate nonresponsive content from the eDiscovery workflow.

Analytics: Through eDiscovery, you can analyze and organize review sets to help reduce the number of documents that you have to review. By grouping related documents into near-duplicate detection groups, your review procedure will become more streamlined. The email threading feature, which identifies specific messages, provides a complete context of a conversation in an email. The themes feature allows you to analyze and organize review sets' themes. It also assigns a theme to each document so that you can easily review related ones. Through analytics, you can improve the efficiency of your review process by allowing reviewers to inspect a fraction of the documents that they have collected.

Computed document metadata: Many of the premium features of eDiscovery, such as analytics and conversation threading, add metadata properties to help review documents. The metadata is made up of details about a specific function that's performed. You can easily filter through the metadata properties of documents to find those that meet your specific criteria. After documents have been exported, the metadata can be used in third-party review software.

Transparency of long-running processes: In eDiscovery, processes that are long-running are usually triggered by user actions. These include adding content to a case, performing analytics, and carrying out search queries. Through the process overview, you can easily track the status of your long-running processes and request support if needed.

Full reporting for all processes: The process report can help you manage various processes, such as searching for and reviewing cases.

Enhanced data source mapping: Users can be searched based on their locations, sorted by sites, and placed in groups based on their activities. You can also explore collaborators and obtain new locations.

Finally, the eDiscovery capabilities of Microsoft Purview provide a comprehensive and robust solution for managing the various aspects of electronic discovery. With the help of tools such as eDiscovery, Content search, and eDiscovery Premium, organizations can easily find, analyze, and extract content from various sources in Microsoft 365. The eDiscovery Premium platform features advanced capabilities such as machine learning, which can help organizations reduce the complexity and cost of their eDiscovery processes.

Microsoft Purview Compliance eDiscovery Features

The comprehensive capabilities of Microsoft Purview's eDiscovery platform make it easy to manage the discovery process. These tools allow organizations to easily find, collect, and export content from various Microsoft 365 platforms, such as OneDrive for Business, Exchange Online, and Microsoft Teams. With the help of its advanced capabilities, such as predictive coding and custodian management and others as below, Microsoft Purview can help organizations comply with legal requirements and efficiently manage their eDiscovery processes.

Case level custodian management: You should manage the individuals who you consider to be the people of interest in a case, also known as custodians. When you add noncustodial data sources and custodians to a case, there's a legal hold that you can place on them. You can then communicate with them and collect content related to the case through the legal hold process.

Error remediation: A process known as error remediation is used to fix various processing errors. The goal of error remediation is to fix the issues that prevent the proper processing of data during the eDiscovery process. For instance, files that are encrypted or have password protection cannot be processed. In error remediation, the affected files are downloaded, and the password-protected ones are removed. The decrypted ones are then uploaded.

Export to customer-owned Azure Storage location: You can export your documents from a review setting to Azure Storage using the company's managed account. Premium eDiscovery allows users to customize the data that they export. This allows users to export various types of documents, such as native and text files, redacted documents, and metadata.

Import non-Office 365 data: Certain documents that need to be analyzed in eDiscovery Premium are not in Office 365. With the import feature of non-Office 365 data in eDiscovery Premium, you can easily send documents that are not in Office 365 to review sets.

Legal hold notifications: Through a legal hold notification, case custodians are instructed to preserve relevant content. You can monitor the status of the notices that they've received and read. With the eDiscovery Premium platform, you can create and send notifications and escalations to case custodians if they fail to acknowledge the hold notification.

Predictive coding models: Reduce the amount of case content by implementing predictive coding techniques. This will help you prioritize the items that need to be reviewed. With the help of predictive coding techniques, you can create and train models that will help you identify the most relevant items for review in a case. The system then applies prediction scores to the various items in the review set. This feature allows you to filter the review set by the prediction score. It will then allow you to focus on the most relevant items.

Integration eDiscovery other solutions: Cases related to **Microsoft Purview Insider risk management solution** can be escalated to other cases in eDiscovery whenever additional legal review is required to determine if there are risks associated with certain activities. The integration between Microsoft's solutions can help both the legal team and the risk management team work more efficiently. It can provide them with a complete view of the activities of their users.

With **Microsoft Copilot**, you can easily create KeyQL search queries in eDiscovery utilizing natural language. Also, with Copilot, you don't need to learn how to create KeyQL queries, know operators, and search metadata fields in order to use it. In a review set, Copilot can provide contextual summaries of most items. These summaries are based on the text that was included in the selected item. Reviewers can quickly identify the information that's useful when exporting or tagging items with this summary. The Copilot for security summary provides a comprehensive view of an item, including attachments, meetings transcripts, and documents.

In conclusion, the integrated features of Microsoft Purview' compliance eDiscovery solution provide a powerful and flexible approach to managing electronic discovery. Through the use of advanced tools, organizations can easily find, collect, and analyze data in Microsoft 365 environments. This ensures that they are following all the necessary legal requirements. The integration of advanced capabilities such as predictive coding and custodian management helps improve the eDiscovery process' accuracy and efficiency. This can also help organizations lower their costs and improve their outcomes.

Attain Compliance with Regulatory Requirements Such as GDPR and CCPA with Microsoft Purview

It can be very challenging for organizations to comply with various regulations such as the GDPR (General Data Protection Regulation) and CCPA (California Consumer Privacy Act). With the help of Microsoft Purview, organizations can easily automate and simplify the various steps involved in complying with regulations. This section will help you implement Microsoft Purview to ensure that your organization is following the regulations of the CCPA and the GDPR.

Data Discovery and Classification

Getting the proper information about where and how your data is stored is the first step toward ensuring that it follows the regulations introduced by the CCPA and GDPR. Both the CCPA and GDPR emphasize how important it is for companies to understand, categorize, and manage their personal information. Through Microsoft Purview, organizations can now automatically categorize and identify sensitive information such as personal health records, financial data, and PII. This solution helps organizations identify and categorize sensitive information based on its regulatory and sensitivity importance. This is a crucial aspect of ensuring that they're following the regulations introduced by both the CCPA and the GDPR.

Through Microsoft Purview, organizations can create and train custom models and data classifiers that can handle various sensitive information types. The General Data Protection Regulation (GDPR) requires organizations to protect the privacy of their customers by implementing policies that allow them to control how their data is used. Through Microsoft Purview's automatic classification and monitoring capabilities, organizations can continuously monitor and analyze their data to ensure that they are taking the necessary steps to protect their customers' privacy.

Data Governance and Management

One of the most critical factors that businesses need to consider when it comes to complying with the regulations of the CCPA and GDPR is having the proper governance in place. With Microsoft Purview, organizations can easily create and manage policies and procedures that govern the use, sharing, and access of their data. The platform's central data governance solution works seamlessly with various Microsoft tools, including Power BI and Azure. Through the platform's ability to create and manage policies across various aspects of an organization's data estate, it helps businesses comply with the regulations laid out by the CCPA and GDPR.

Through its built-in governance tools, Purview helps organizations manage the access to sensitive data they collect. These tools can be used to define roles and responsibilities for users, restrict access based on the business need, and ensure that only authorized individuals have access to that data. Additionally, it can help organizations implement automated data deletion and retention policies in line with the regulations of the GDPR and the CCPA. It helps organizations implement policies that are consistent across their data repositories. This ensures that they follow the regulations laid out by the CCPA and GDPR.

Data Mapping and Data Subject Rights

The CCPA and GDPR require companies to provide individuals with certain rights regarding the use and disclosure of their personal information. These include the ability to access, correct, and delete their data. The GDPR allows people to ask for more information about the kind of personal data that an organization collects and uses. The California Consumer Protection Agency (CCPA) also provides residents with the right to know the types of information that are collected and used.

Through Microsoft Purview, organizations can create comprehensive data lineage reports and data maps that help them identify where and how their customers' information is being used. This solution helps organizations comply with the requirements of the CCPA and GDPR by quickly and efficiently processing requests for access to their customers' data. With the help of automated workflows, organizations can now process and present their data in a manner that's compliant with the regulations.

The requirements of the GDPR and the CCPA involve keeping records of how organizations process and share information. With the ability to track the movement of data across multiple systems, Microsoft Purview helps organizations meet the regulatory requirements and provide effective responses to inquiries.

Risk and Compliance Management

The Microsoft Purview platform provides advanced compliance and risk management capabilities, which help organizations manage their data handling and security risks. These are areas of focus under the CCPA and GDPR. The regulations place a heavy emphasis on preventing unauthorized access and use of sensitive data. They also require organizations to promptly notify regulators about breaches. With the Purview Compliance Manager, organizations can continuously monitor and assess their compliance with regulations and manage their risks.

With the built-in capabilities for managing compliance, the Compliance Manager in Purview can help organizations comply with key regulations such as the EU's General Data Protection Regulation and the CCPA. Through its library of controls, the Purview platform can help organizations continuously monitor their compliance with legal requirements. With the help of the Compliance Manager, organizations can easily track and report on their progress toward meeting the legal requirements related to data protection.

Through its data loss prevention capabilities, Microsoft Purview can help organizations safeguard sensitive information. Through a data loss prevention policy, organizations can prevent unauthorized access and use of sensitive information such as credit card details and Social Security numbers. This capability helps organizations comply with the requirements of the CCPA and GDPR regarding protecting personal information.

Data Protection and Encryption

The CCPA and GDPR require organizations to implement suitable measures to safeguard the personal data they collect. For instance, the GDPR requires organizations to encrypt and pseudonymize their personal data in order to prevent unauthorized access. On the other hand, the CCPA requires companies to implement effective security measures to safeguard the information they collect. Through Microsoft Purview, an organization can implement information protection solutions that are integrated with its platform. These solutions provide a level of security that is designed to protect the sensitive data that it collects.

Through Microsoft Purview, organizations can implement policies that are based on their classification to ensure that sensitive data is protected. Also, through its information protection solutions, Microsoft can provide organizations with a level of control over how their data is accessed. The data minimization principle of the GDPR applies to organizations. This means that they have to limit access to the personal information that they collect. With the help of Purview, an organization can enforce this by restricting the access to sensitive data to only those individuals who have the necessary clearance.

Incident Response and Breach Management

Both the CCPA and the GDPR require organizations to notify authorities about data breaches within a certain time frame. The former also requires that consumers be notified if their information has been exposed. Through its platform, Microsoft Purview, organizations can easily identify and respond to data breaches. It features a variety of tools that can help them detect anomalous activities that can indicate a breach. With the help of Microsoft Purview, an organization can generate reports that detail the details of a data breach, such as the number of affected individuals, the nature of the incident, and the steps taken to address it. These reports can help minimize penalties.

Conclusion

Due to the increasing number of regulations and laws regarding data privacy, it is important that organizations are able to comply with the latest legislation such as the CCPA and GDPR. Through Microsoft Purview, organizations can easily manage their compliance efforts by delivering a comprehensive suite of tools that help them find, classify, protect, and monitor their data.

The ability to integrate with other infrastructure and automate compliance tasks makes Microsoft Purview an ideal tool for organizations that are looking to comply with the new regulations. With the help of Microsoft Purview's suite of tools, organizations can efficiently manage their data privacy and ensure transparency, all while reducing their risk of penalties and improving their reputation as data keepers.

With this, we have come to the end of this chapter. In the chapter, we have covered the various aspects of compliance, such as Communication Compliance, data lifecycle management compliance or managing information protection, records management, and eDiscovery. Finally, we have used these concepts to ensure that organizations are following the requirements of the CCPA and GDPR. In the next chapter, we will take deep dive into information security and privacy requirements using Microsoft Purview.

CHAPTER 8

Information Security in Microsoft Purview

In the previous section, we talked about some of the key aspects of compliance, including data lifecycle management, eDiscovery, and communication. We have also utilized these concepts to help organizations comply with the requirements of the General Data Protection Regulation (GDPR) and the CCPA. In the upcoming section, we will delve into the details of information security regulations utilizing Microsoft Purview.

In this chapter, we cover information security solution of Microsoft Purview, which are as follows:

- Microsoft Purview information protection solution

- Microsoft Purview data loss prevention

- Microsoft Purview Insider risk management

- Information barriers solution of Microsoft Purview

- Microsoft Purview privileged access management

Initially, we have a brief overview of all the above solutions, but further, we will have detail understanding of information protection and information barriers (IB) solutions in this chapter.

© Charles Waghmare 2025
C. Waghmare, *Introducing Microsoft Purview*,
https://doi.org/10.1007/979-8-8688-1204-0_8

Introduction

With Microsoft Purview data security solution, you can manage and safeguard your information. This chapter will introduce you to the various features of Microsoft Purview data security software. It will also help you identify and implement effective security measures for your organization. Every organization has to protect its data. Having the proper strategy and resources is very important to ensure that your information is protected. Through Microsoft Purview information protection, you can discover, classify, and safeguard sensitive data residing anywhere.

Your company's data may be stored in various cloud services and on-premises equipment. This could be accessed through Microsoft 365 and other online services. One of the most critical steps in protecting your information is identifying which items are most sensitive. Custom expressions or built-in functions can help identify sensitive data types. Instead of identifying the components of an item, a trained classifier can use data examples to identify sensitive information. Data classification is a process that helps identify sensitive data types in an organization. It can also help visualize the actions that your users are taking with these types of items.

Microsoft Purview information protection solution has various features that can help safeguard your data in various locations. Aside from being able to protect data, sensitivity labels also provide a way to interact with other features of Purview. Administrators and users can easily identify the sensitivity of their data by using sensitivity labels. These labels can be used to implement various protection actions, such as visual markings, access restrictions, and encryption.

One of the most important factors that you can consider when it comes to protecting your data is encryption. This process involves converting your data into ciphertext. Ciphertext is different from plaintext in that it cannot be used by computers or people unless it is decrypted. An encryption key is required for decryption. It ensures that only authorized users can access your content. With Microsoft Purview Double Key Encryption, sensitive data will be protected from the strictest security standards. With Microsoft Purview Customer Key, you can easily meet regulatory and compliance requirements when it comes to managing root keys. You can explicitly grant Microsoft 365 services access to your encryption keys for various cloud-based services, such as antimalware and eDiscovery. The unauthorized sharing of sensitive information can have detrimental consequences for your organization. It may violate regulations or laws.

Through **Microsoft Purview data loss prevention**, you can protect your organization's sensitive information from accidental or unintentional sharing. A data loss prevention policy is designed to help prevent unauthorized access to and use of sensitive information. It includes a list of the information that you want to keep protected. To identify and prevent unauthorized access to sensitive information, you should monitor the activities of your devices and services. The appropriate conditions must be met to implement a policy on certain items, such as driver's licenses, credit cards, or Social Security numbers. When a match is found, blocking an activity or audit is performed. An override procedure is also used to block the activity.

The **Microsoft Purview Insider risk management** solution provides a comprehensive view of your organization's risk behaviors. It allows you to quickly identify and resolve these issues. Through the use of logs from Microsoft 365, and Microsoft Graph, you can define policies that identify risk indicators and take action to address them.

The **information barriers solution of Microsoft Purview** allows you to restrict the communication between users and groups within Microsoft Teams, OneDrive, and SharePoint. Information barriers (IB) are commonly used in regulated industries to prevent conflicts of interest and ensure the confidentiality of internal data.

Some users may be able to access sensitive information in Microsoft Exchange without being restricted. This could allow them to carry out internal threats or compromise accounts. With the help of **Microsoft Purview privileged access management**, you can protect your company from breaches and comply with best practices by restricting the access of sensitive data. Instead of having constant access, just in-time access rules are used for certain tasks.

Information Protection

Through Microsoft Purview information protection, you can identify, classify, and safeguard sensitive data in various environments. This solution gives you the necessary tools to protect your data and prevent it from getting damaged. The information protection tools included in Microsoft Purview will allow you to know your data, protect your data, prevent your data, and govern your data as shown in Figure 8-1.

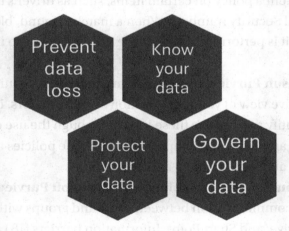

Figure 8-1. *Microsoft Purview information protection tools*

Following Figure 8-1, let's have a look at each capability of information protection solution part of Microsoft Purview.

Know Your Data

- This capability helps to identify sensitive information through using custom scripts of built-in functionality. Evidence drawn through this capability are keywords, confidence levels, and proximity.

- Instead of finding patterns in an item, a trainable classifier can identify sensitive data by analyzing examples of the data that you're interested in. Classifiers can be created and trained using your own content or built-in methods.

- A data classification process is used to identify the various types of items in an organization. It can help identify those that have a retention label or sensitivity label. Through this information, you can analyze your users' actions when it comes to these items.

Protect Your Data

- A sensitivity labeling solution is a way to protect your sensitive data as it travels across various devices and apps. Examples of scenarios include protecting sensitive data in emails and documents, safeguarding calendar items, and keeping chat and meetings private.

- With Microsoft Purview information protection client solution for Windows computers, one can extend labeling to File Explorer and PowerShell.

- It is mandatory for organizations to maintain encryption keys within geographical boundaries. This ensures that only authorized individuals can decrypt protected content.

- With message encryption, you can protect the contents of emails and other attachments sent to users on different devices. It prevents unauthorized access. For instance, if you want to restore an encrypted email, you can use message encryption.

- Service encryption with a customer key can protect the data of users in Microsoft data centers from unauthorized access. It complements BitLocker encryption.

- SharePoint information rights management (IRM) protects libraries and lists in Microsoft SharePoint. It ensures that only authorized individuals can access and use the downloaded files.

- Rights management connector is a protection-only solution for on-premises deployment of Exchange or SharePoint servers. It can also be used for file servers that use the FCI.

- Information protection scanner discovers, labels, and secures sensitive data in a data center.

- For cloud-based applications, Microsoft Defender finds, labels, and secures sensitive information stored in data centers.

- In Microsoft Purview data maps, automatic labeling is performed on sensitive information in the assets. This includes files and databases in Azure Data Lake or Azure Files, as well as schematic data in Azure Cosmos DB and SQL DB.

Prevent Data Loss

- To prevent unauthorized access to sensitive data, below features aims to encrypt transmission.

- Microsoft Purview data loss prevention tool can help prevent the accidental sharing of sensitive information. Windows 10 users can now benefit from the extension of its data loss prevention feature to include devices that are used and shared.

- The Chrome extension from Microsoft Purview can now be used to add protection against data loss.

- The ability to protect data in various types of files and folders through on-premises repositories is now available with Microsoft Purview. This feature allows users to monitor and protect file shares and SharePoint folders and document libraries.

Govern Your Data

- **Microsoft Purview data lifecycle management** (formerly Microsoft information governance) allows organizations to manage their data in Microsoft 365. It includes a variety of retention labels that allow you to retain or remove content.

- Microsoft information governance allows mailbox content to be archived after an employee leaves the company which can be accessed by compliance officers, records managers, and administrators.

- For archived mailboxes, users can also benefit from the added storage space provided by archive mailboxes.

- The file plan allows you to create and import labels in bulk or export them for analysis. It also supports various administrative features to help you track and identify business requirements.

- Supports various types of retention labels for different items or policies, and flexible schedules for deletion and retention. These can be applied automatically or manually.

- Before you permanently delete content, it can be reviewed and documented for proof of its disposition.

Information Barriers

With Microsoft 365, organizations and groups can collaborate and communicate with each other across various platforms. It also allows users to restrict the communication of certain groups depending on their needs. This can be used to prevent conflicts of interest between the two groups or when it's necessary to limit the collaboration and communication between them. Sometimes, this scenario can also include restricting the collaboration and communication between certain members of an organization to ensure the safety of its internal data.

In addition, the company's information barriers (IB) are supported in various platforms, such as OneDrive for Business, SharePoint Online, and Microsoft Teams. An IB or compliance administrator can create policies that prevent or allow certain groups from communicating with each other within Microsoft Teams.

An organization should utilize an IB policies as follows:

- Members of the day trader group should refrain from sharing or communicating with the marketing team.

- Teachers in a certain school should not be permitted to share or communicate educational materials with pupils in another institution.

- Employees who are involved in the confidential operations of a company should refrain from exchanging files or collaborating with certain groups.

- Members of an internal team that holds trade secrets should avoid communicating or calling other users in groups within the firm.

- Research teams should only communicate with the product development group through online channels.

Information Barriers with Microsoft Teams

Information barriers are policies that determine and prevent unauthorized collaboration and communication within Microsoft Teams such as follows:

- Randomly search for any user

- Kickstart a random chat session with anyone

- Kickstart a group chat session

- Invite some colleagues to join a meeting

- Share screen whenever possible

- Sharing of files

- Access to files through its URL

Users who perform certain activities within Microsoft Teams may not be able to proceed after being included in an information barriers policy. An information barriers policy can also block the communication between users in Microsoft Teams who are included. The users who are affected by the information barriers policy may be removed from the group chat or team sessions they are part of.

A policy known as a Purview information barrier is a set of policies that can be used by an admin to prevent groups or individuals from communicating with one another. An information barrier can be useful when one of the departments is handling data that should not be shared with other units. An information barrier can also be useful when a group wants to be kept apart from people outside of it. Information barriers are included in Microsoft Teams to help support shared channels. An information barrier can also be used to restrict the sharing of certain types of information.

The primary driver of information barrier comes from financial services sector. The Financial Industry Regulatory Authority, (FINRA) reviews and addresses conflicts of interest among members of the industry. It also provides guidance on managing such conflicts. Although IB were initially introduced to the financial services industry, they have also been used in other areas such as below:

- In the education sector, students from one school may not be able to look up the details of their classmates from other schools.

- Prevent unauthorized access of client data by lawyers for different firms.

- Government access and limited control over information access in various groups and departments.

- In the professional services industry, groups of people are only permitted to talk to certain customers through the use of guest access during an engagement.

- For instance, if an organization has a policy that blocks the communication between two groups, then the members of the strategy department and Marketing department can't talk to each other. However, they can still communicate with HR as shown in Figure 8-2.

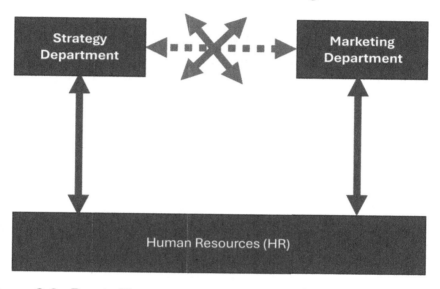

Figure 8-2. *Due to IB, two groups cannot collaborate with each other*

IBs can be utilized in scenarios such as the members of a team are prohibited from communicating with or sharing information with another group. They must also refrain from sharing data with individuals outside of the group. A policy evaluation service can determine if a message complies with the requirements of an IB.

Information Barrier Triggers

The following events trigger the activation of the IB policies.

Members are added to a team: When a user is added to a team, their policy should be evaluated against the policies of the other members. After the user has been added, they can perform all their assigned tasks without

any additional checks. The user would not be displayed in the search
results if their policy prevented them from joining the team as shown in
Figure 8-3.

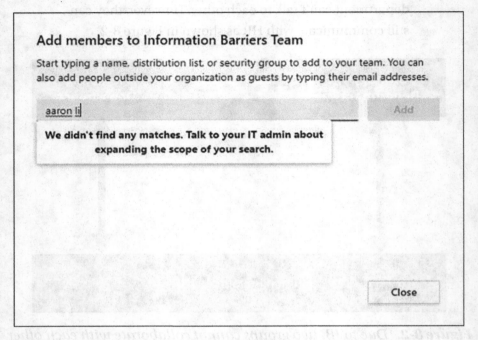

Add members to Information Barriers Team

Start typing a name, distribution list. or security group to add to your team. You can
also add people outside your organization as guests by typing their email addresses.

aaron li   Add

We didn't find any matches. Talk to your IT admin about
expanding the scope of your search.

Close

Figure 8-3. *IB activation when members are added to a team*

A new chat is requested: The chat is analyzed whenever a user requests
a new one. The goal is to make sure that the discussion doesn't go against
an IB policy. If a discussion goes against an official IB policy, it will not be
started as shown in Figure 8-4.

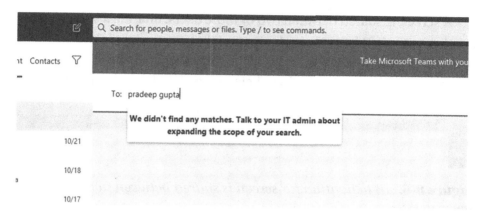

Figure 8-4. *IB activation for 1:1 chat*

A user is invited to join a meeting: When a user is invited to participate in a meeting, the policies related to that individual are evaluated against those related to the other team members. If a violation has occurred, the user will not be allowed to participate in the meeting as shown in Figure 8-5.

Figure 8-5. *IB activation for user invited to join meeting*

189

A screen is shared between two or more users: Sharing a screen with another user must be evaluated to ensure that it does not violate the other users' IB policies. Screen sharing will be disallowed (shown in red box in Figure 8-6) if the other users' IB policies are violated.

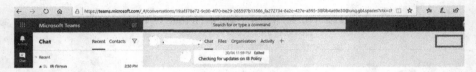

Figure 8-6. *IB activation for screen is shared between two or more users*

A user places a phone call in Teams: Voice calls made using VOIP are evaluated to make sure that they do not violate the team's policies. If there is a violation, the call will be blocked.

Guests in Teams: To manage the access of guests in your organization, go to the Groups section of Microsoft 365.You can then define the policies for the IB by making sure that all guests are discovered.

Impact of IB on Existing MS Teams Chats

The policy administrator of the information barrier can make changes to a policy, or it can be activated after a user's profile has changed. The evaluation service then searches the members to make sure that they don't violate the rules. If a new policy is implemented or an existing one is changed, the evaluation service will check whether the existing communication between users is allowed to continue.

1:1 chat: If two users are no longer communicating due to an application or a policy that blocks it, then further communication will be stopped. Their existing chats will only be read-only as shown in Figure 8-7.

Figure 8-7. *IB activated to block specific user in 1:1 chat*

Group chat: If a user's participation in the group chat violates the policy, they may be removed from the discussion. The other users who joined without following the rules may also be banned from the chat. Although the user can still see past conversations, they will not be able to participate in new ones. If a new policy that blocks communication is implemented to more than one user, it may lead to the removal of those affected by it from the group chat. Although the user can no longer participate in new conversations, they can still view past ones as shown in Figure 8-8.

Figure 8-8. *IB activated to block specific user in a group Chat*

Also, user cannot send messages to a group chat as shown in Figure 8-9:

Figure 8-9. *IB activated prohibits user from sending message in a group chat*

Conclusion

Users can't join ad hoc meetings post activation of IB policies; users are not allowed to participate in meetings if the meeting roster exceeds the limit for attendance. The issue is that the checks conducted by the IB rely on whether or not a user can join a meeting chat. This means that only those who can be added to the roster will be allowed to participate. When a user adds another user to the meeting roster, the number of people participating in the meeting immediately increases. The meeting's attendance limit will be exceeded, and new participants will not be allowed to join.

New users will not be allowed to join the meeting if the chat roster is full. This applies to everyone who is not already on the roster. If the meeting's chat roster is full and the Internet bridge is not enabled, new users may still participate in the meeting. But they won't be able to access the chat option. To accommodate new users, the meeting's roster should be temporarily removed from inactive members. In the future, we plan to expand the scope of the meeting chat rosters.

Users can't join channel meetings, if an IB policy is enabled, channel meetings are not allowed to be attended by users who are not part of the team. The main issue is that the IB checks determine whether a user can join a meeting. They only allow people who can be added to the meeting roster. The channel meeting's chat feature is only available to members of the team and channel itself. Nonmembers cannot access or participate in the chat. If an organization has an IB policy enabled, a nonteam member can't join a channel meeting if they try to do so. If an organization does not have an IB policy enabled, a nonteam member can still join a channel meeting if they try. However, they will not be able to access the chat feature.

IB policies don't work for federated users; if you allow your organizations to have federated relationships with external entities, then those users will not be restricted by the policies of the IB. On the other hand, if you allow users to interact with each other through meetings or chats organized by external users, then those policies will not prevent communication between the entities.

Information Barriers with OneDrive and SharePoint Online

Below information barriers determine and prevent unauthorized collaboration in OneDrive and SharePoint:

- Add member to a site

- Sites access or content by a user

- Sharing site content with another user

- Using site search

OneDrive can support various information barriers (IBs) modes as below:

- When a site's nonsegmented users provide their OneDrive, its IB mode is automatically set to open.

- In the case that a site's owner or moderator facilitates collaboration between incompatible users using OneDrive, its owner-moderated mode is automatically set.

- Within 24 hours of enabling a user to provide their OneDrive, the site automatically sets its IB mode to explicit and user will be associated with their OneDrive.

- When a site allows a user to share their OneDrive with unsegmented users, its IB mode is set to mixed. This mode is an opt-in option that the site's admin can configure for the user.

Information barriers (IBs) can be used with SharePoint to restrict access to certain parts of the site. There are three types of modes supported: explicit, implicit, and open explained below:

- When a SharePoint site does not have subsites, its IB mode will automatically be set to open.

- When a site is created to allow users to work together with incompatible segments, its owner-moderated IB mode should be applied.

- When a site is made available by Microsoft Teams, its IB mode is set to implicit. This means that a Global Administrator or a SharePoint Administrator cannot manage sections with this configuration.

- If a site is created by an end user or a SharePoint Administrator and a segment is added to it, its explicit mode is automatically set.

Privileged Access Management

Some users may have stood access to certain sensitive information in Microsoft Exchange Online, which could allow them to compromise accounts or carry out internal threats. With the help of privileged access management, Microsoft can protect organizations from breaches and meet their compliance goals by restricting the standing access to critical settings and data. Just-in-time access controls are implemented to allow only authorized users to access certain tasks. With the help of privileged access management, organizations can operate without standing privileges in Microsoft 365. It can also provide them with a layer of protection against unauthorized access.

Layers of Protection

The ability to manage privileged access provides additional security features and data protection in Microsoft 365. With the ability to manage privileged access, a security model can be created that protects sensitive information and the configurations of Microsoft 365. Figure 8-8 shows how privileged access can be managed in Microsoft 365. It builds on the security model that was previously provided for the platform. With the ability to manage privileged access, a security model can be created that protects sensitive information and the configurations of Microsoft 365 as shown in Figure 8-10.

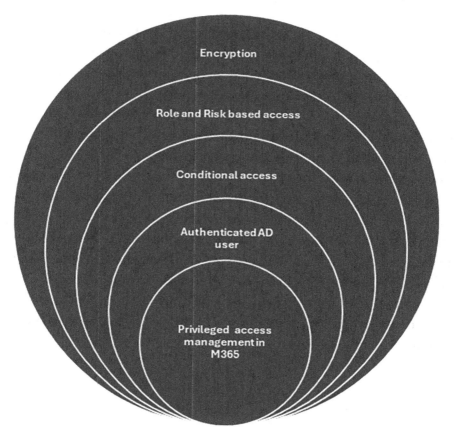

Figure 8-10. *Privileged access management in M365*

With the help of privileged identity management, users can easily monitor and control the access to critical resources within their organization. This service is part of Microsoft Entra ID, and it can also be used with other Microsoft services such as Azure and Intune.

Microsoft's privileged access management framework is designed to provide a level of protection that's focused on the task level. On the other hand, Entra's identity management platform allows users to manage their identity and access to various tasks. Entra's platform mainly handles the management of access for role groups and AD roles. On the other, Microsoft Purview privileged access management system only applies to tasks.

Enabling privileged access management while already using Microsoft Entra privileged identity management: With the ability to manage privileged access, Microsoft 365 data can be more secure. It also provides a level of protection that's focused on the task level.

Enabling Microsoft Entra privileged identity management while already using Microsoft Purview privileged access management: By integrating Entra's privileged identity management platform with Microsoft Purview privileged access framework, organizations can extend the privileges of their users to data residing outside of Microsoft 365.

With this, we have come to the end of the chapter. In this chapter, we covered information security solution of Microsoft Purview, which are information protection solution, data loss prevention, Insider risk management, information barriers, and Purview privileged access management. In the next chapter, we will be talking about best practices for effective information governance by sharing industrial best practices around information governance.

CHAPTER 9

Best Practices for Effective Information Governance

In the previous chapter, on the information security and privacy, we have seen to how to manage security and privacy requirements using Purview, and during this, we covered recommendations while implementing information security measures, protecting sensitive information assets, and enforcing encryption and access controls. In this chapter, we will cover strategies for optimizing data management practices using Microsoft Purview, best practices for effective information governance using Microsoft Purview, and Microsoft Purview information governance success stories.

Strategies for Optimizing Data Management Practices Using Microsoft Purview

Data management is essential for organizations to ensure compliance, maintain operational effectiveness, and maximize the value of their information. With Microsoft Purview, they can easily implement and manage a comprehensive set of tools and features designed to improve

© Charles Waghmare 2025
C. Waghmare, *Introducing Microsoft Purview*,
https://doi.org/10.1007/979-8-8688-1204-0_9

their practices. This section offers a variety of strategies and tips to help organizations implement and manage their data management efforts as shown in Figure 9-1.

Figure 9-1. *Strategy pillars*

Develop a Unified Data Governance Strategy

A comprehensive data governance strategy is needed to ensure consistency across an organization. With Microsoft Purview, organizations can manage their data assets more effectively. This includes tools such as data cataloging and classification. Your data governance strategy should clearly state the goals of improving its quality and security. It should also help ensure regulatory compliance. Using Purview's data catalog feature will allow you to create a central repository of your data assets. It should include information lineages, data classifications, and metadata. Using Purview's policy management tools, you can create and enforce policies related to data governance, such as access controls and data retention.

Regularly update and review policies to keep up with changes in the requirements of the business and regulatory environment. To keep up with the changes brought about by the regulations and business needs, policies should be regularly reviewed and updated. Gather stakeholders from different departments to ensure that the policies are aligned with the company's objectives.

Implement Effective Data Classification

Classification is a process that enables organizations to manage their data based on its importance and sensitivity. With Microsoft Purview, they can easily categorize their data and apply appropriate privacy and security measures.

A framework for data classification can be created that divides information into various categories depending on its sensitivity. These include restricted, confidential, and internal. With the help of Purview's automated tools, organizations can easily apply labels to their data based on its metadata and content. This ensures that the classifications are accurate and consistent across the organization. Regularly update and review data classifications to keep them up-to-date and relevant to the changes in regulatory requirements and data sensitivity.

Coordinate with stakeholders and data owners to create frameworks that are aligned with business requirements and regulatory guidelines. Regularly carry out audits to ensure that classifications are correct and address any issues.

Enhance Data Lineage and Traceability

Data lineage is a process that involves the flow of information from one source to another. It is often used to track data transformations and improve the efficiency of data management. With Microsoft Purview, organizations can visualize and analyze their data lineage.

Through the use of Purview's data lineage features, users can visualize and analyze the various components of their data. This helps them understand how their data is used and processed. Ensure that the data lineage information is updated regularly to reflect the changes in the integration and processing of information. Doing so can help maintain current and accurate records. Analyzing the data lineage can help identify potential issues related to changes in the sources, transformations, or integrations of information. It can also help ensure that the records are secure.

To ensure that their data is accurate and complete, organizations should involve data analysts and engineers in mapping their lineage. Using lineage visualizations can also help them analyze and make informed decisions.

Implement Data Quality Management Practices

Data quality is a vital part of any organization's operations and should be regularly monitored and assessed. With the help of Microsoft Purview, you can improve the quality of your data.

To ensure the quality of data, establish a set of metrics and standards that will help measure its completeness, consistency, and accuracy. These standards should also be used to set performance goals. Purview's tools for data quality assessment can help you monitor and analyze the quality of your data. They can identify and address various issues related to its quality, such as duplicates, missing values, and inconsistencies. You should create and implement procedures for data enrichment, cleansing, and validation. Automated workflows should be employed for data management.

Coordinate with business users and data stewards to define standards for data quality to meet the needs of the organization. Metrics and reports can be used to track progress and identify areas where more improvement can be made.

Optimize Data Access and Security

Data management involves ensuring that the efficient and secure access to information is maintained. With Microsoft Purview, you can manage access controls and safeguard sensitive information.

You must define policies that specify who has access to the data and how they can modify or share it. You can also implement RBACs to ensure that users are given appropriate privileges based on their roles. Use Purview's features to implement various security measures to safeguard sensitive data. These include masking, encryption, and other measures. You must also ensure that the practices related to data security are in line with industry best practices and regulatory requirements. You should regularly examine and report on the activities related to data access. With the help of Purview's reporting and monitoring tools, you can monitor and identify unauthorized access attempts and breaches.

Regularly update and review access control policies to align them with the organization's security and needs. Based on the least privilege principle, implement access controls to reduce the likelihood of unauthorized access.

Foster Data Stewardship and Accountability

Responsible management of data assets is an essential part of effective data stewardship. With Microsoft Purview, you can easily manage and monitor your data assets.

Designate data owners or stewards who will oversee the management of your data assets. They should have clear roles and responsibilities. Create and implement procedures for data stewardship, such as data ownership and data quality management. You can also use Purview's features to support these activities. The goal of effective data stewardship is to establish a culture of accountability. This can be achieved by establishing clear roles and responsibilities for those involved in the management of data.

Data stewards should be provided with training to help them understand their duties and roles. Regularly assess the effectiveness of your data stewardship procedures and identify areas for potential improvement.

Support Compliance and Regulatory Requirements

One of the most critical factors that businesses consider when it comes to managing their data is ensuring that their practices follow the regulations. With Microsoft Purview, they can easily manage their compliance efforts.

Understanding the various regulations that affect data management is very important for any organization. In addition to creating and implementing policies, this process also involves addressing the various regulations related to data protection and accessibility. With the help of Microsoft Purview's compliance tools, businesses can monitor and report on their data protection measures and usage. They can also create and maintain reports that detail their compliance practices.

Ensure that your compliance department and legal team are engaged in creating and implementing policies that comply with regulations. Regularly conducting audits of your compliance procedures can help identify any gaps and ensure adherence.

Enhance Data Integration and Interoperability

Integrating data is a vital part of creating a cohesive view of information across various systems. With Microsoft Purview, you can easily find, catalog, and integrate data.

Using Purview's integration capabilities, you can easily connect and integrate data sources, such as databases and cloud platforms. You should also ensure that the integration processes are reliable and efficient. Ensure that your data is compatible with other applications and systems. Using Purview's metadata management and data catalog features can help you do this. You should regularly assess and evaluate the effectiveness of your data integration efforts to identify potential issues and address them accordingly.

In addition to data engineers, you should also enlist the help of integration specialists to create and implement effective integration strategies. Tools and frameworks can help automate and streamline integration efforts.

Promote Data Literacy and Training

Getting the most out of your data is very important, and training and data literacy are two of the most crucial factors that people should consider. Microsoft Purview has a variety of resources that can help them improve their skills.

To help individuals become knowledgeable about the various features of Microsoft Purview, such as data management techniques, policies, and tools, training programs can be created. They can also be provided with ongoing support to keep them informed about updates. People can enhance their data literacy by leveraging Purview's tutorials, support, and documentation. Encourage them to explore and utilize these resources to learn more about data management. Support the development of data literacy by organizing data-related initiatives, such as workshops, webinars, and events that promote data sharing and knowledge exchange.

To ensure that the training programs are relevant and effective, they should be tailored to the specific requirements of the users. Regularly update and evaluate the training materials to keep up with the changes in the Purview features and practices.

Monitor and Optimize Data Management Processes

One of the most critical factors that businesses need to consider when it comes to improving their data management processes is continuous monitoring. With Microsoft Purview, they can analyze and monitor their data management activities.

Purview's reporting and monitoring tools can help organizations identify and monitor key metrics related to their data management efforts. They can then be used to evaluate and improve their performance. Regularly audit data management procedures to ensure their compliance with regulations and policies. These findings can then be used to improve the data management process. Follow best practices and leverage the features of Purview to improve the efficiency of your data management processes.

To ensure continuous improvement and optimization, it's important that the data management process undergoes a regular review cycle. In order to gather insights and feedback during the optimization process, engage both the data management and stakeholder groups.

Leverage Automation and Advanced Analytics

Advanced analytics and automation can help organizations improve their data management processes and provide them with more insight. Microsoft Purview provides these capabilities.

With Purview's automation features, you can easily automate various data management tasks, such as data classification and data cataloging.

This can help reduce the amount of manual work and improve the efficiency of your organization. With the help of advanced analytics, you can gain deeper insight into your data's usage and quality. You can then make informed decisions and improve the efficiency of your data management efforts. You can now integrate Purview with various analytical tools and platforms to enhance their capabilities and provide you with more insight into your data. This will allow you to make more informed decisions and improve the efficiency of your data management efforts.

To maximize the impact and efficiency of your data management efforts, identify and prioritize the various tasks that can be automated. To ensure that your automation models and workflows are up to date and aligned with the latest requirements of data management, regularly review them.

Foster Collaboration and Communication

Communication and collaboration among various stakeholder groups are necessary for successful data management. With Microsoft Purview, users can easily access tools that help them manage their data.

To establish effective communication channels, regular meetings and discussions about data management issues should be organized. The use of Purview's collaboration features can help facilitate the coordination among various stakeholder groups. Cross-functional collaboration is also needed to ensure that the various teams and departments work together seamlessly on the management of data. This can be done by facilitating the development of policies and practices. To promote a culture of knowledge exchange, it is important that organizations document and publicize their best practices and success stories about data management.

With the help of collaboration features in Purview, data management teams can easily communicate and coordinate with one another. Feedback and suggestions from stakeholders can help ensure that data management techniques are in line with the company's needs.

Develop and Implement a Data Management Framework

A data management framework helps organizations manage their data. Through the tools and features of Microsoft Purview, they can implement and manage these frameworks.

A good data management framework should be created to describe the various steps involved in managing an organization's data assets. It should also contain components such as data quality and security. Using Purview's features and tools will help organizations implement a data management framework. They should also ensure that it is integrated with existing systems and practices. Make sure that the framework is regularly monitored and refined. You should also gather feedback from the data management team and other stakeholders to find areas for improvement.

Involve the various stakeholder groups in the development and implementation of the framework. Doing so will ensure alignment with the company's objectives and needs. Regularly update the framework to reflect changes in the requirements and practices of data management.

Conclusion

Using Microsoft Purview will let you optimize your data management techniques. This approach involves utilizing the platform's features and toolsets. It will help you create a single data governance strategy, classify and trace data, enhance traceability and lineage, and focus on data quality management. Various strategies can also be used to enhance the efficiency and effectiveness of your data management efforts. These include developing a data stewardship strategy, fortifying regulatory compliance, fortifying interoperability and data integration, promoting data literacy training, and utilizing advanced analytics and automation.

One of the most critical factors that businesses consider when it comes to data management is the establishment of a framework that will allow them to collaborate and communicate with their stakeholders. This approach can help them achieve their goals and improve the efficiency of their operations. Microsoft Purview is a powerful platform that can help organizations improve their data management efforts. Through its various features, it can help them create a single data governance strategy, improve visibility into their data, and achieve their goals.

Best Practices for Effective Information Governance Using Microsoft Purview

Effective information governance is crucial for managing data assets, ensuring compliance, and maintaining data integrity across an organization. Microsoft Purview offers a comprehensive suite of tools and features that support robust information governance. By leveraging these tools and adhering to best practices, organizations can enhance their data governance strategies and achieve better outcomes. This extensive section outlines best practices for using Microsoft Purview to implement effective information governance.

Define Clear Governance Objectives and Scope

Prior to implementing Microsoft Purview information governance software, it is important that the company has clear goals and objectives. This step will help guide the process and ensure that the framework adheres to the organization's priorities. Understanding the various

207

requirements of the business will help you make informed decisions. Before you start implementing Microsoft Purview information governance software, it is important that you thoroughly assess the requirements of the business. This step will help you make informed decisions and ensure that the framework adheres to the organization's priorities. A governance strategy should be created that clearly states the scope and goals of the efforts involved in controlling information. These include data quality, classification, regulatory compliance, and security.

Develop a Comprehensive Data Catalog

A well-designed data catalog is a vital component of an organization's information governance strategy. It helps organizations identify, manage, and secure their data assets. Microsoft Purview's platform provides a comprehensive repository that enables organizations to manage their data assets efficiently. With the help of Purview's data cataloging capabilities, you can easily identify and categorize data sources across your organization. You should also ensure that the catalog includes data lineage information and metadata. Make sure that the data catalog has clear categories and tags so that users can easily find and access the information they need.

Implement Robust Data Classification

A vital part of information governance, data classification enables organizations to determine and manage information based on its importance and sensitivity. Microsoft Purview's features allow organizations to segment and categorize data using predefined schemes. A data classification framework should be designed to meet the security and privacy requirements of an organization. It should also include categories for various types of data. Using Microsoft Purview's classification tools, organizations can apply labels to their data assets based on their metadata and content. They should also regularly update their policies to reflect changes in the business needs and regulatory requirements.

Establish Data Governance Policies and Procedures

Data governance is a process that involves the establishment and enforcement of policies that define the proper management and protection of information. With Microsoft Purview, you can create and enforce policies that are designed to help organizations achieve this. Create comprehensive policies that cover various aspects of data protection, accessibility controls, retention, and quality standards. These should be aligned with industry best practices and regulatory requirements. Using Purview's policy management tools, create and enforce policies for data assets. You should also regularly review and update them to keep them relevant.

Enable Data Lineage and Traceability

Data lineage is a process that enables organizations to identify and manage the flow of information from their origin to their destination. With Microsoft Purview, they can visualize the various elements of this process. Through the use of Purview's data lineage features, users can visualize the various steps involved in the data flow process. This visibility allows them to make informed decisions and improve their efficiency. To ensure that the information in the data lineage is up-to-date and accurate, it's important that the company regularly updates its records.

Implement Data Access Controls

When it comes to protecting sensitive data, it is important to have policies in place that restrict who can access it. With Microsoft Purview, organizations can easily implement and enforce these policies. A good access control policy should specify who can access and modify the data assets. It should also be implemented with a role-based access control to ensure that the appropriate user is granted access based on their responsibilities. With the help of Purview's access control features, organizations can easily monitor and manage their data access permissions. They should also regularly review these policies to make sure that they are in line with the company's security and needs.

Ensure Data Quality and Integrity

Data quality is an essential part of an organization's information governance strategy. With Microsoft Purview, you can manage and monitor its data quality. Assess the quality of data by implementing metrics and standards. Then, use Purview's tools to identify and resolve issues related to data quality. To ensure that your data meets quality standards, establish processes that involve data cleansing, enrichment, and validation. Regularly update and review your practices to accommodate the changing needs of your data management.

Support Compliance and Regulatory Requirements

One of the most critical factors that businesses consider when it comes to information governance is compliance with regulations. With Microsoft Purview, they can manage their compliance by monitoring their data usage and ensuring that their information is protected. In order to comply with regulations such as the Health Insurance Portability and Accountability Act of 1996 (HIPAA), the General Data Protection Regulation (GDPR), and the Credit Protection and Compliance Act (CCPA), organizations must first identify and document the relevant requirements. With Microsoft Purview, organizations can monitor and analyze their data usage and develop reports that detail their compliance with regulations. They can also regularly update their practices to ensure that they are in line with the latest legislation.

Foster Data Stewardship and Accountability

Responsible management of data assets is a critical part of an organization's information governance strategy. Having the right data governance practices and procedures is very important to ensure that the information is protected. Microsoft Purview provides a variety of features that help organizations manage their data. To ensure that the information is protected, an organization should assign data owners or data stewards to oversee the management of its assets. They should have clear roles and responsibilities. Through Microsoft Purview's data governance tools, you can easily track and document the activities of your data stewards. It also helps in establishing a culture of accountability.

Promote Data Literacy and Training

In order to ensure that individuals have the necessary knowledge and skills to comply with information governance policies, training and data literacy are crucial. Microsoft Purview offers a variety of resources and tools to help individuals improve their data literacy skills. To help individuals become knowledgeable about data management methods, policies, and Microsoft Purview's tools, training initiatives are planned. Users will also be provided with ongoing support and updates. To help individuals improve their data literacy skills, create and maintain documentation and resources using the governance and data catalog features of Microsoft Purview.

Monitor and Audit Data Governance Activities

One of the most critical factors that businesses need to consider when it comes to data governance is regular monitoring and reporting. With Microsoft Purview, they can easily create and manage reports that detail their activities. To ensure that their data is being properly managed, businesses need to establish processes that are designed to monitor and audit their activities. With Purview's auditing and monitoring features, they can easily identify potential issues and create reports. Regularly auditing data governance procedures can help businesses identify areas of their operations that need improvement. Furthermore, using audit findings, they can enhance their policies and procedures in an effort to refine them.

Leverage Automation and Advanced Analytics

Advanced analytics and automation can help improve the information governance process by allowing organizations to gain deeper insight into their data. Microsoft Purview provides these capabilities. Through the use of automation features, Microsoft Purview can help organizations improve the efficiency of their data governance processes by reducing manual work and enhancing the data classification and metadata extraction process. Through the use of advanced analytics, Microsoft Purview can help organizations identify trends and gain insight into their data. This can then be used to make better decisions and improve the efficiency of their information governance processes.

Integrate with Other Data Management Tools

Integrating Purview with other platforms and tools can help improve data governance by allowing users to see all of the activities related to data assets. It also helps with better coordination across different systems. Integrating Purview with other tools and platforms can help improve data governance. It can also help ensure that the integration supports a consistent and seamless flow of information. By integrating Purview with other platforms, you can synchronize the policies and activities related to data governance. This will help establish a comprehensive approach to managing information.

Establish a Data Governance Framework

A framework that provides a defined structure and guidelines for managing the activities related to data governance is an ideal tool for organizations. With Microsoft Purview, they can easily implement and manage frameworks. A framework for data governance should be created and implemented to define the roles and responsibilities of individuals and organizations in managing the data governance process. It should also contain components such as data stewardship and quality management. Use Purview's governance features to implement the framework, such as data cataloging and policy management. It should also be regularly updated and reviewed to reflect the changes in the requirements of the organization.

Foster Collaboration and Communication

Data owners, business users, and data stewards need to work together and communicate effectively in order to ensure that information governance is effective. Through Microsoft Purview, they can access tools that help them manage their data. To encourage collaboration, establish channels

213

and hold regular meetings to talk about policies, updates, and data governance issues. The use of Purview's collaboration features can also help data owners and managers coordinate. By involving different groups in the creation and implementation of practices and policies related to data governance, a culture of collaboration can be established. Their input should be incorporated into the guidelines.

Conclusion

Using Microsoft Purview will require an organization to adopt a comprehensive approach to information governance. This can be done through the development of a data catalog, the establishment of policies, and the robust classification of data. In addition to having a comprehensive approach to information governance, organizations should also adopt best practices that help with the creation and maintenance of a data quality environment. These include the establishment of policies and procedures, the monitoring and auditing of activities, and the use of advanced analytics and automation.

In addition to utilizing Microsoft Purview, an organization can also integrate it with other tools and create a framework for data governance. This approach will help it attain better information management results, ensure data integrity, and comply with its corporate objectives. Microsoft Purview offers a powerful platform that enables organizations to effectively implement information governance. Through its features and best practices, it can help them improve their data visibility, gain more control over their data, and achieve more favorable business outcomes.

Microsoft Purview Information Governance Stories

The Microsoft Purview data governance solution helps organizations manage and protect their information assets. It includes a variety of features such as classification, data cataloging, and compliance. This report aims to highlight the various success stories that have been achieved by organizations using the platform. In the section, we will see masked success stories of Microsoft Purview from retail corporation, healthcare provider, and financial services firms.

Financial Services Firm: Enhancing Compliance and Data Security

Background: Due to the complexity of the global financial services industry's data collection and management, a prominent organization had to find a solution that would allow it to maintain regulatory compliance while protecting its sensitive information. The company had a hard time managing its data due to its lack of visibility into its lineage, data silos, and the challenges in ensuring regulatory compliance while protecting sensitive information.

Solution: The organization had to implement Microsoft Purview to solve these issues. Through its data classification and data cataloging features, the company was able to automate the process of identifying and securing sensitive information across various systems. Its ability to provide a clear view of the data lineage allowed the company to improve its impact analysis and track its progress.

The company was able to attain greater control over the usage and access of its data, which helped facilitate its compliance with regulations. Moreover, the automated labeling and classification of data allowed it to protect and manage sensitive information according to the regulations.

The company implemented Microsoft Purview's data protection features to secure its sensitive information. These included access controls and encryption. The organization was able to improve its data management and efficiency by implementing automated classification and cataloging processes. These helped reduce manual tasks and improve the efficiency of its operations.

The implementation of Microsoft Purview solution allowed the company to enhance its data security and comply with regulations. It also helped it improve its operational efficiency by reducing manual tasks.

Healthcare Provider: Improving Data Quality and Integration

Background: A large healthcare organization is needed to improve the efficiency and effectiveness of its data management processes. The company had a variety of challenges in terms of data quality, visibility, and integration. The organization encountered issues such as fragmented information sources, poor data quality, and limitations in integrating patient information from different systems. These factors inhibited its ability to make informed decisions and improve operational efficiency.

Solution: Microsoft Purview was selected to help the organization address these issues. Its integration and data cataloging capabilities allowed the organization to create a single view of its patient data across multiple systems. Its ability to automate data quality monitoring and lineage tracking also allowed the organization to improve its efficiency.

The use of Purview's tools for data quality management allowed the organization to attain better consistency and accuracy in its patient information. Through automatic assessments, the organization was able to identify and address issues that affected the data. By utilizing Purview's integration capabilities, a healthcare organization was able to attain a comprehensive view of its patient information, facilitating efficient and

216

coordinated care. By having better integration and visibility into its data, the organization can now generate actionable insights that can improve its operational performance and patient outcomes.

Healthcare organizations can now achieve better operational efficiency, decision-making capabilities, and patient care through the use of Purview.

Retail Corporation: Streamlining Data Governance and Compliance

Background: A global retailer faced the challenge of managing and securing the massive amount of customer and sales information that it collects from various sources. The organization needed a robust solution that would allow it to comply with regulations and ensure data governance. The organization had difficulty with data governance due to various issues, such as the lack of visibility into its data lineage and inconsistent management practices.

Solution: The organization was able to implement Microsoft Purview to resolve these issues. Through its data classification and cataloging features, the company was able to gain a central view of its sales and customer information. It also gained insight into its data lineage, which allowed it to comply with data protection regulations. The Purview solution allowed the organization to manage its data assets more effectively. It also established consistent practices for data management, which improved the quality of its data. Through the implementation of Purview's compliance management tools, the retailer was able to meet various regulatory requirements and safeguard its customers' data. The integration of data governance and data management practices led to better decision-making and efficiency. With a clear view of data, the company was able to capitalize on its insights to improve customer experiences and grow its business.

The features of Microsoft Purview helped a retail organization simplify its data management and regulatory processes. This led to better operational effectiveness, data management, and regulatory compliance. With this, we have come to the end of this chapter.

Post covering strategies for optimizing data management practices using Microsoft Purview, elaborating best practices for effective information governance using Microsoft Purview and description of Microsoft Purview information governance success stories, we are concluding this chapter. In the next chapter, we will focus on future trends in information governance. With this focus, we will share future insights in information governance with emerging technologies and trends shaping information governance, role of AI and machine learning in information governance, and predictions for the future of information governance and compliance.

CHAPTER 10

Future Trends in Information Governance

We have arrived in the final chapter of the book, and through a learning journey, we conclude this chapter with innovative thinking around future trends in the information governance. In the previous chapter, we have discussed about strategies for optimizing data management practices using Microsoft Purview, elaborating best practices for effective information governance using Microsoft Purview and description of Microsoft Purview information governance success stories. In this chapter, we will be discussing possible future trends in information governance, role of artificial intelligence (AI) and machine learning (ML) in information governance, and predictions for the future of information governance and compliance using Microsoft Purview to create innovate experience for the end users.

Introduction

Certainly! Exploring the future of information governance is a complex and nuanced topic that spans technological advancements, evolving regulatory landscapes, and shifts in organizational priorities. Here, we delve into an extensive analysis of future insights in information governance, examining emerging trends, anticipated challenges, and strategic opportunities that

© Charles Waghmare 2025
C. Waghmare, *Introducing Microsoft Purview*,
https://doi.org/10.1007/979-8-8688-1204-0_10

will shape the field. This exploration will cover a broad range of topics, including technological innovations, regulatory changes, data ethics, and organizational strategies, with a focus on how these factors will influence the evolution of information governance.

Information governance is undergoing a transformative shift driven by rapid technological advancements, increasing regulatory demands, and the growing recognition of data as a critical strategic asset. As organizations continue to generate and manage vast amounts of data, effective governance practices become crucial in ensuring data quality, security, compliance, and utilization. This comprehensive analysis explores the future of information governance, providing insights into key trends, challenges, and strategies that will define the landscape over the coming years.

Future Trends in Information Governance

As organizations navigate an increasingly complex digital landscape, the future of information governance is evolving rapidly. Information governance, a critical discipline that encompasses the management, protection, and utilization of data, is undergoing transformative changes driven by technological advancements, shifting regulatory landscapes, and growing demands for data ethics and transparency. These future trends are shaping how organizations approach data management, ensuring they can leverage data as a strategic asset while adhering to regulatory and ethical standards. Let's look into some of the possibilities in the future trends of information governance. Trends lies in the following areas: role of AI and ML in information governance, predictions for the future of information governance and compliance, collaboration with blockchain, and IoT and ethical considerations in data management as shown in Figure 10-1.

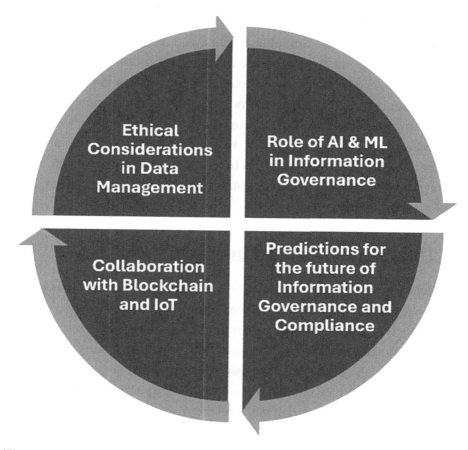

Figure 10-1. *Possible future trends in Information Governance*

Integration of Artificial Intelligence and Machine Learning

The rise of artificial intelligence (AI) and machine learning (ML) is expected to transform the way information is managed. These technologies can help improve the quality of data by allowing organizations to automate and enhance its classification, anomaly detection, and assessment.

221

Through the use of AI and ML, tools can automatically categorize and catalog data based on its content, metadata, and context. This method can reduce the manual work required in the classification process and ensure that the data is accurately labeled. ML can analyze large data sets to find anomalies, patterns, and possible issues. This capability can help organizations maintain strict data quality standards and proactively address issues related to its integrity. An organization can identify possible security threats or compliance issues by analyzing anomalous usage and access patterns in its data. Predictive analytics can help prevent such issues from escalating.

Big Data Analytics and Insights

Big data analytics is becoming more prevalent as organizations look to gain deeper insight into their data. With the help of advanced tools, they can then make more informed decisions and improve their efficiency. A big data platform can provide real-time analytics, which lets an organization monitor and analyze data continuously. This capability can help them respond more quickly to changing situations and make better decisions.

There are two types of analytics: prescriptive and predictive. The former uses models that predict future outcomes and trends, while the latter provides recommendations based on them. With the help of these tools, organizations can make informed decisions and improve their efficiency. A good data visualization tool can present complicated information in an interactive and intuitive manner, which helps improve accessibility and enables better comprehension of data insights.

Blockchain and Decentralized Data Management

The rise of blockchain technology and the increasing number of data management systems that are decentralized are making it possible to ensure the security and integrity of information. Through immutable records, which are resilient to tampering, blockchain technology can ensure the authenticity and integrity of data. This is particularly beneficial for organizations that need to maintain a transparent and secure record-keeping process.

By implementing distributed ledger technology, data sharing will be conducted efficiently and securely across numerous parties without the need for a central authority. This facilitates more trustworthy and collaborative ecosystems. A smart contract is a type of contract that can automate the execution of transactions and data-related agreements. It can also help boost the efficiency of an organization's operations.

Regulatory Trends and Compliance

Data privacy regulations are becoming increasingly stringent as governments and regulatory bodies seek to protect individuals' personal information. Organizations must stay informed about evolving regulations and implement robust compliance measures. **General Data Protection Regulation (GDPR):** The GDPR has set a high standard for data protection and privacy in the European Union. Future regulations may build upon GDPR principles, introducing new requirements for data consent, access, and protection. **California Consumer Privacy Act (CCPA):** The CCPA and its amendments, such as the California Privacy Rights Act (CPRA), provide additional rights and protections for California residents. Organizations operating in California must ensure compliance with these regulations. **Global Data Protection Standards:** As data protection concerns are not confined to specific regions, global standards may emerge to harmonize data privacy regulations across jurisdictions. Organizations operating internationally will need to navigate these standards and ensure global compliance.

Data ethics is becoming a critical component of information governance, addressing concerns related to the responsible use of data, bias, and fairness. Ethical data usage by organizations must ensure that their data practices align with ethical principles, such as respecting individuals' privacy and avoiding discriminatory practices. Developing ethical guidelines and frameworks will be essential for responsible data management. With **bias and fairness**, AI and ML algorithms are increasingly used in decision-making processes, addressing biases and ensuring fairness in data-driven outcomes becomes crucial. Organizations must implement practices to identify and mitigate biases in algorithms and data models. With transparency and accountability, organizations are expected to provide transparency in their data practices and be accountable for their data-related decisions. This includes disclosing how data is collected, used, and shared and ensuring that data practices align with the ethical standards.

Data Stewardship and Management

Data stewardship is critical for ensuring the effective management and governance of data assets. The role of data stewards will continue to evolve as organizations place greater emphasis on data quality, security, and compliance. Data stewards will be responsible for maintaining high standards of data quality, including implementing data quality frameworks, monitoring data integrity, and addressing data quality issues. Data stewards will manage data access controls, ensuring that data is accessible to authorized users while protecting sensitive information from unauthorized access. Data stewards will play a key role in fostering collaboration among stakeholders, including IT, legal, and business teams. Effective communication and coordination will be essential for implementing data governance practices and addressing emerging challenges.

Information governance will increasingly be integrated with broader business functions and strategies, aligning data management practices with organizational goals and objectives. As organizations undergo digital transformation, data governance will be aligned with initiatives such as cloud adoption, automation, and data-driven innovation. Effective data governance will support and enhance digital transformation efforts. Data governance practices will be integrated with customer experience strategies to ensure that customer data is managed effectively and utilized to improve interactions and engagement. Information governance will support operational efficiency by streamlining data management processes, optimizing data integration, and enhancing data accessibility for decision-making and analysis.

The rise of data-as-a-service (DaaS) models is transforming how organizations access and utilize data. DaaS platforms offer on-demand access to data and analytics services, enabling organizations to leverage external data sources and capabilities. DaaS models provide cost-effective and scalable solutions for data management, reducing the need for extensive internal infrastructure and resources. Organizations must implement governance frameworks to manage their relationships with DaaS providers, ensuring that external data sources meet quality and security standards. Effective vendor management practices will be essential for ensuring that DaaS providers adhere to contractual obligations, data protection requirements, and service level agreements.

Data Democratization and Literacy

Making data and analytics widely accessible would democratize it, empowering employees to make informed decisions. To ensure that they have the necessary skills and knowledge to utilize this information, organizations should provide training and support. In order to ensure that data is secure, accurate, and compliant, organizations must adopt policies and procedures related to data governance. These include establishing access controls, enforcing stewardship practices, and building frameworks for data quality. A culture centered around data should also be fostered to enable data democratization. Data must be regarded as a strategic asset, and organizations should foster a culture that encourages decision-making with the help of data.

The ability to understand and use data is known as data literacy, and organizations must enhance this skill in order to take advantage of its strategic value. Implementing training programs on this subject can help workers improve their skills and enable them to make more informed decisions. Data visualization tools and resources can help employees improve their data literacy skills by making complex information more understandable. This process is an ongoing initiative, and organizations must continuously invest in training opportunities to keep their staff members up to date with the latest techniques, tools, and trends.

Managing Data Complexity and Scale

Big data is becoming more prevalent, and organizations will need to manage the various challenges associated with it. To effectively handle the growing volume of information, they will need to adopt advanced platforms and technologies. Getting a unified view of data from different sources is challenging, and integrating information from different systems and sources will help. Tools and techniques for data integration will make it easier to access and use, and organizations can automate such processes to handle the growing amount of data.

The future of information governance involves the development of adaptable frameworks that can accommodate the varying needs of companies and their business objectives. These frameworks should be able to handle the increasing amount of data and regulatory requirements. Organizations can also invest in solutions and technologies that can handle the growing volume of information. Modular and cloud-based data management solutions can handle the scalability requirements. Organizations must adopt a culture of continuous learning to adjust to the changes brought about by the evolution of information management technologies and practices. They should also regularly review their strategies to ensure that they remain relevant and effective.

Collaboration and Partnership

As organizations expand their data ecosystems, they will need to work with external partners and vendors to ensure that the exchange of information is secure and compliant. This can be done through the establishment of data sharing agreements. These agreements should cover the various details of the exchange of information, such as the access and protection of the data. Working with industry groups and regulatory bodies can help organizations develop effective data governance policies and navigate the changes brought about by the regulations.

Data governance involves building trust with stakeholders, and organizations must ensure that they are transparent with how they gather, use, and share information. This can help improve the confidence of customers, regulators, and partners. Responsibility for data-related practices and decisions should be established to ensure that the organization upholds its commitments and addresses any issues that may arise. Enhancing credibility and trust by addressing ethical issues in data management can be achieved by implementing guidelines and principles.

Conclusion

The information governance framework will undergo significant changes due to various factors, such as technological advancements and the increasing emphasis on data stewardship and ethics. As a result, organizations will need to devise innovative approaches to effectively utilize, manage, and protect their information assets.

Some of the key factors that will influence the development and implementation of information governance in the future include the integration of machine learning and artificial intelligence (AI), the rise of blockchain technology, and the increasing scrutiny on data ethics and privacy. In addition, organizations will have to address issues related to data complexity and scalability, as well as foster a culture of data literacy and democratization. To effectively utilize and manage their information assets, organizations will have a need to continuously monitor and address the various factors that affect their information governance. This can help them improve their performance and enable them to capitalize on the full potential of the data they collect.

Role of Artificial Intelligence (AI) and Machine Learning (ML) in Information Governance

The concept of information governance refers to the process of ensuring that information is properly managed and utilized to meet regulatory and organizational requirements. Traditional methods of handling data are being challenged due to its increasing complexity. With the emergence of AI and ML, the process of information governance can be automated, improved, and optimized. The section explores the diverse applications and roles of ML and AI in information management. It also covers the challenges and potentials of these technologies.

Introduction to AI and ML in Information Governance

The rise of artificial intelligence (AI) and machine learning (ML) has created new opportunities for information governance. AI is a type of computer that mimics the human intelligence that is used to think and learn. On the other hand, ML is a subset that focuses on the ability to improve the performance of systems by learning from data. These technologies can help organizations improve their data management and make informed decisions. They can also help them comply with regulations.

AI is made up of various technologies that are designed to mimic the cognitive functions of humans, such as reasoning and learning. In the realm of information governance, this technology is utilized to model and analyze data efficiently.

ML is a branch of AI that deals with the creation of algorithms that can be used to make predictions and decisions based on information. These models are ideal for various tasks, such as analyzing and mapping complex data sets.

Enhancing Data Management with AI and ML

Automated data classification is a key component of information governance that uses ML and AI. Traditional methods of classification tend to involve manual categorization and tagging, which can lead to errors. Through the use of machine learning algorithms, a classification system can be trained to identify patterns and characteristics in data. It can then apply these rules to new data. This method can reduce the need for manual work and ensure that the data is accurate and consistent. Natural language processing, also known as NLP, is a subfield of AI that focuses on analyzing and understanding human language. It can be used to classify various types of data, such as social media posts and emails.

The metadata collection is a vital part of information management, as it provides information about a data's usage and origin. With the help of AI and ML, it can be enhanced to automate the enrichment and tagging processes. Through the use of AI and ML, automated classification can be performed on data by generating metadata tags based on their content and context. For instance, financial documents can be tagged with relevant terms such as "invoices," "expenses," or "revenue." Artificial intelligence can enhance the metadata of a data by providing context-rich information such as its usage patterns and data lineage. This process can then be used to improve the data governance by allowing a more accurate view of its interactions.

Through the use of AI and ML, organizations can easily integrate and aggregate data from various sources. This allows them to gain a comprehensive view of their information. An AI program can link and match a data source's information by identifying similarities between its elements. An AI system can also consolidate customer information from different databases. ML models can also perform data transformation, which involves converting data from various structures and formats into a single format. This simplifies the integration process and increases the quality of data.

Improving Data Quality with AI and ML

High data quality is essential for organizations to make informed decisions and improve their operational efficiency. Machine learning and AI can help them achieve this by automating various validation and cleansing processes. AI systems can detect and correct various errors, such as duplicates and inaccuracies, in data. For instance, ML models can identify anomalies in customer information or financial transactions. Artificial intelligence can also enhance the quality of data by incorporating data from other sources. For example, it can provide a more complete understanding of a customer's profile by analyzing information from public records or social media.

By utilizing ML models, organizations can predict future outcomes and trends based on historical data. ML algorithms can analyze past data to identify trends and patterns, which enables companies to make predictions about upcoming events like sales or the behavior of consumers. AI can then be used in risk management to identify possible risks by analyzing patterns in data. For instance, it can help predict supply chain disruptions.

Enhancing Data Security and Compliance

ML and AI can help improve data security by allowing organizations to identify and respond to threats. An AI program can identify unusual usage or access patterns in a data set. For instance, it can detect anomalous data transfers or login attempts, which could help alert to potential security breaches. A behavioral analytics system uses AI to analyze user behavior and detect deviations from the norm. This capability can help organizations identify malicious activities and insider threats.

One of the most critical factors that information governance needs to consider is the compliance with regulations. With the help of AI and ML, it can automate and streamline the process of monitoring and reporting. AI can help organizations monitor and report on their data to ensure that they're following various regulations, such as the Health Insurance Portability and Accountability Act of 1996 (HIPAA), the General Data Protection Regulation (GDPR), and the California Consumer Protection Act (CCPA). Through the use of AI, it can also create and maintain audit trails, which are documents related to the usage, access, and changes of data. These records can be used to support regulatory reporting.

Supporting Data Governance and Stewardship

ML and AI play a vital role in the creation and implementation of efficient data governance systems. Through the use of AI, it can help in the creation and implementation of data governance policies, such as identifying areas where the access controls should be strengthened or where there are issues with data quality. AI-based tools and insights can help data stewards manage their assets. Through the use of machine learning, they can analyze and monitor data usage, quality, and compliance to ensure that the goals of data governance are met.

Through the use of AI and ML, data discovery and management processes can be improved, making it easier to manage and find information. Through the use of AI and ML, data discovery can be automated, allowing organizations to create a comprehensive catalog of their data. This process can help improve the accessibility and visibility of their information. A contextual search engine, powered by AI, helps users find relevant data sets based on their queries and contextual information. It also enhances data discovery and offers efficient retrieval.

Facilitating Data-Driven Decision-Making

ML and AI can help improve the presentation and interpretation of data, giving users actionable and intuitive information. AI-driven tools for data visualization and analysis provide users with an interactive view of their information. They can explore data trends and narrow down on specific metrics to gain insights that can help them make informed decisions. Artificial intelligence (AI) can also help data scientists identify trends and opportunities in their data. This can help them make informed decisions and improve the efficiency of their operations.

ML and AI can help organizations make informed decisions by delivering prescriptive and predictive analytics. A predictive analytics model predicts the future based on historical data. It can be utilized by decision-makers to make informed decisions and anticipate trends. A prescriptive analysis is a process that recommends the best actions based on the collected data. With the help of AI, it can also suggest strategies to improve the efficiency of an organization or mitigate risk.

Future Potential and Developments

The developments in machine learning and artificial intelligence will likely shape the future of information governance. The developments in ML and AI will lead to enhanced algorithms that can improve data quality, security, and management. The innovations in AI techniques like reinforcement learning and deep learning will also affect information governance. Due to the increasing number of applications and technologies that are integrated with artificial intelligence and machine learning, the development of information governance will become more sophisticated.

As the technologies that are used for artificial intelligence and machine learning continue to develop, the ethical and regulatory standards will also undergo change. The regulations and standards that will be used to manage the use of artificial intelligence and machine learning will undergo change. Organizations must be aware of these developments and be able to comply with them. The evolution of ethical guidelines for the use of AI and ML will help organizations manage the implications of these innovations and foster responsible data governance.

In conclusion, the rise of machine learning and artificial intelligence (AI) has revolutionized the way information is managed. These technologies are capable of improving the quality and accuracy of data, but they also expose organizations to ethical and privacy issues. As the evolution of ML and AI continues, their increasing role in data governance will lead to new innovations and the creation of new opportunities for organizations. Effective use of these technologies will enable organizations to navigate the challenges of managing data efficiently.

Predictions for the Future of Information Governance and Compliance Using Microsoft Purview

The future of information governance and compliance is increasingly intertwined with advanced technological solutions, particularly those offered by platforms like Microsoft Purview. As organizations continue to navigate the complexities of managing vast amounts of data, ensuring compliance with evolving regulations, and safeguarding against data breaches, the role of integrated solutions like Microsoft Purview becomes pivotal. This analysis explores predictions for the future of information governance and compliance, focusing on how Microsoft Purview and similar platforms are likely to shape these domains over the coming years.

Intelligent Data Classification and Tagging

The integration of AI and machine learning in the classification and labeling of data is anticipated to have a major impact on how information is managed. Future developments in AI will enable Purview to gain a deeper understanding of the context of data. This will allow it to more accurately categorize and tag data. This will allow organizations to manage their data according to their business needs and regulatory requirements. Through the use of machine learning, Purview will be able to continuously improve its classification capabilities by learning from the data patterns and interactions that it encounters. This will allow the company to adapt to new regulations and business requirements.

Automated Risk Assessment and Management

Future compliance strategies will rely on AI-powered risk assessments. Microsoft Purview will use AI to proactively identify and resolve potential breaches. Through advanced predictive analytics, Purview can predict future compliance risks and help organizations identify potential issues before they happen. In the event of a compliance issue or data breach, Purview will use AI to automate the process of identifying and assessing the affected data, as well as recommend remediation steps, which can significantly reduce the response time and minimize the risk of damage.

Compliance with Emerging Regulations

As the world moves toward more stringent privacy laws, Microsoft Purview will be a vital part of helping organizations manage these changes. Through its global regulatory adaptation, Microsoft Purview will help organizations manage the changes brought about by the GDPR, the CCPA, and the DSA. This will include features that help them comply with these regulations. Through its automated policy updates, Microsoft Purview will help organizations continuously update their policies to comply with the latest regulations. This will allow them to remain compliant without having to manually implement changes.

Enhanced Data Sovereignty and Localization

Due to the increasing number of requirements for localization and data sovereignty, Microsoft Purview is developing solutions that will help organizations manage their data in certain regions. Future updates will include geographic controls that will allow organizations to enforce and manage data sovereignty rules. Through Purview, they'll be able to ensure that their data is stored and processed in accordance with local regulations. Through the new capabilities of Purview, organizations will be able to easily create and manage reports that comply with local regulations. This will allow them to demonstrate their adherence to the regulations and privacy laws in their local area.

Advanced Data Encryption and Protection

Microsoft Purview will continue to focus on data security. It will lead the way in developing new methods and techniques for protecting and encrypting data. In the future, Microsoft Purview will introduce advanced encryption protocols designed to ensure that sensitive information remains secure both in transit and at rest. This feature will help address the increasing concerns about unauthorized access and data breaches. In addition, through the use of AI, Purview will be able to detect and respond to various threats in real time, helping to reduce the likelihood of breaches and improve data security.

Data Integrity Monitoring

As organizations expand their data volumes, they will need to ensure that the integrity of their data is maintained. Through Purview, they will be able to manage and secure their data. Through Purview, organizations will be able to continuously monitor and analyze their data for any issues that could affect its integrity. This will help them detect unauthorized changes, anomalies, and discrepancies. Through its integration with blockchain technology, Microsoft Purview will be able to provide more effective and secure ways to store and manage data. This will also help organizations maintain transparency and security.

Comprehensive Data Cataloging and Discovery

Microsoft Purview will allow for enhanced data governance through improved discovery and cataloging. Through a unified data catalog, Purview will allow organizations to manage and govern their data assets across various systems and sources. This will help them make informed decisions and improve their efficiency. Through advanced search and discovery capabilities, users will be able to find and access information more quickly. With the help of artificial intelligence, Purview will allow them to find information based on its content, metadata, and context.

Data Stewardship and Ownership

In order to ensure proper data governance, it is important that the ownership and stewardship of information are carried out properly. With Purview, this will be supported through advanced tools. Through role-based access controls, Purview will allow organizations to set and enforce policies for data access based on the responsibilities and roles of their users. This will help prevent unauthorized access and ensure that data is only accessible to authorized individuals. In the future, Purview will also feature a dashboard that will allow data stewards to monitor and manage their data assets. This will help them ensure that they are following proper policies and that they are getting the most out of their data.

Integration with Emerging Technologies

As organizations expand their use of hybrid and cloud computing, Microsoft Purview is well-positioned to support them. Through its integration with various cloud platforms, including Amazon Web Services, Google Cloud, and Azure, Purview will be able to provide organizations with a more effective way to manage their data. Purview will be able to help organizations manage their hybrid data by providing tools that allow them to keep track of their data across both cloud and on-premises environments. These tools will include features for enforcing policies and ensuring compliance.

Collaboration with Blockchain and IoT

The rise of IoT and blockchain technologies will have a significant impact on how organizations manage their data. Through its partnership with these new technologies, Microsoft Purview aims to help organizations improve the efficiency of their data management. Through its partnership with blockchain technology, Microsoft Purview will be able to provide its customers with secure and immutable records of their data transactions. This will help them ensure that their data is protected from unauthorized access. As the number of devices using the Internet of Things (IoT) increases, Purview will be able to provide its customers with tools that help them manage and govern the data collected by these devices. These tools will include features that allow them to track the flow of data and secure sensitive information.

Enhanced User Interfaces and Dashboards

Microsoft Purview will focus on enhancing the user experience, with a particular emphasis on providing adaptable dashboards and intuitive interfaces. As part of its continuous efforts to improve the user experience, Microsoft Purview will also release new features that will make it easier for its users to manage their data. These new features will include a variety of customizable dashboards and streamlined workflows. New features will allow users to explore and generate reports using interactive dashboards. In addition, Purview will integrate tools that will make its governance features more user-friendly.

Training and Support

Getting the most out of Microsoft Purview requires knowledgeable support and training. Through its training programs, Microsoft Purview will provide its users with the necessary tools and resources to effectively utilize its features. Through its enhanced support services, Microsoft Purview can provide its users with prompt assistance and guidance. These include phone, chat, and email channels. These will help them resolve their issues and take advantage of its features.

Ethical Considerations in Data Management

As the field of data management continues to evolve, it is important that companies take the necessary steps to ensure that their data is ethically managed. Microsoft Purview will help organizations meet these goals. Through Purview, organizations will be able to manage their data privacy and consent ethically. This includes features that allow them to secure their personal information and obtain and manage user consent.

It is important that companies maintain transparency in their data practices to build trust and comply with regulations. Through Microsoft Purview, organizations can now track and maintain the lineage of their data, keep track of changes in the data, and maintain transparency in their governance. These tools can help them build trust with their stakeholders.

Conclusion

The rapid emergence and evolution of new technologies such as artificial intelligence and machine learning (ML) are expected to transform the way organizations manage their data. With the help of Microsoft Purview, they can now achieve effective compliance and data management. As these innovations continue to expand, the company will also play a vital role in addressing the various challenges that will arise in the future. Through the use of Purview, organizations can now achieve effective information governance and ensure compliance with regulations. The company's ongoing development will also help drive innovation and establish new standards for the management of data.

With this, we have come to the end of this chapter where we have seen the possible future trends in information governance using AI, ML, and blockchain technologies. We also discussed the role of artificial intelligence (AI) and machine learning (ML) in information governance, enhancing information management with AI and ML, improving information quality with AI and ML, enhancing information security and compliance, and finally facilitating information-driven decision-making. Finally, we discussed predictions for the future of information governance and compliance using Microsoft Purview where we foresee intelligent information classification and tagging, automated risk assessment and management, automated compliance with emerging regulations with continuous update of Microsoft policies, and finally, encryption and protection with advanced security protocols of Microsoft.

Index

A, B

C

© Charles Waghmare 2025
C. Waghmare, *Introducing Microsoft Purview*,
https://doi.org/10.1007/979-8-8688-1204-0

K

L

M

governance, 198, 199
integration/interoperability, 203
pillars, 198, 199
quality management, 200, 201
reporting/monitoring tools, 204
stewardship, 201, 202

training/literacy, 203
update/review policies, 199

V, W, X, Y, Z

Viva Engage retention policy, 95, 96

Printed in the United States
by Baker & Taylor Publisher Services